FROM A DOGSLED HOLIDAY TO A SAFARI IN DARKEST ONTARIO

Canada offers an incredible array of traveler's treats. And now Gerry Hall, travel writer and editor for the Toronto *Star*, has created the perfect guide to 101 of the most unusual vacation possibilities you're likely to find anywhere. With him you will journey to a church haunted by one of Florence Nightingale's nurses, dine on sumptuous lobster suppers, go bird-watching on Grand Manan, tee off at a golf course where the action begins at midnight, root for your favorite in the World Championship Bathtub Race, and revel in the excitement of the Quebec Winter Carnival. Places, events, activities, transportation, accommodations and meals are all highlighted in this unique handbook to a country full of vacation pleasures you'll never forget.

OFFBEAT CANADA

Bestsellers from SIGNET

- [ ] **NOT AS A STRANGER by Morton Thompson.** (#E9527—$2.95)
- [ ] **THE CRY AND THE COVENANT by Morton Thompson.** (#J7813—$1.95)
- [ ] **THE CARETAKERS by Dariel Telfer.** (#E9485—$2.25)*
- [ ] **TRANSPLANT by Len Goldberg.** (#J9412—$1.95)
- [ ] **PACIFIC HOSPITAL by Robert H. Curtis.** (#J9018—$1.95)*
- [ ] **COMA by Robin Cook.** (#E9756—$2.75)
- [ ] **SPHINX by Robin Cook.** (#E9194—$2.95)
- [ ] **THE YEAR OF THE INTERN by Robin Cook.** (#E7674—$1.75)
- [ ] **INTENSIVE FEAR by Nick Christian.** (#E9341—$2.25)*
- [ ] **'SALEM'S LOT by Stephen King.** (#E9827—$3.50)
- [ ] **THE STAND by Stephen King.** (#E9828—$3.95)
- [ ] **THE SHINING by Stephen King.** (#E9216—$2.95)
- [ ] **CARRIE by Stephen King.** (#E9544—$2.50)
- [ ] **THE DEAD ZONE by Stephen King.** (#E9338—$3.50)
- [ ] **NIGHT SHIFT by Stephen King.** (#E9746—$2.95)

* Price slightly higher in Canada

Buy them at your local bookstore or use this convenient coupon for ordering.

THE NEW AMERICAN LIBRARY, INC.,
P.O. Box 999, Bergenfield, New Jersey 07621

Please send me the SIGNET BOOKS I have checked above. I am enclosing
$_____ (please add 50¢ to this order to cover postage and handling).
Send check or money order—no cash or C.O.D.'s. Prices and numbers are
subject to change without notice.

Name _____

Address _____

City_____ State_____ Zip Code_____

Allow 4-6 weeks for delivery.
This offer is subject to withdrawal without notice.

OFFBEAT CANADA

101 Unusual Vacation Adventures

By
Gerry Hall

A SIGNET BOOK
NEW AMERICAN LIBRARY
TIMES MIRROR

NAL BOOKS ARE AVAILABLE AT QUANTITY DISCOUNTS WHEN USED TO PROMOTE PRODUCTS OR SERVICES. FOR INFORMATION PLEASE WRITE TO PREMIUM MARKETING DIVISION, THE NEW AMERICAN LIBRARY, INC., 1633 BROADWAY, NEW YORK, NEW YORK 10019.

Copyright © 1981 by Gerry Hall

All rights reserved

SIGNET TRADEMARK REG. U.S. PAT. OFF. AND FOREIGN COUNTRIES
REGISTERED TRADEMARK—MARCA REGISTRADA
HECHO EN CHICAGO, U.S.A.

SIGNET, SIGNET CLASSICS, MENTOR, PLUME, MERIDIAN AND NAL BOOKS are published by The New American Library, Inc.,
1633 Broadway, New York, New York 10019

First Printing, April, 1981

1 2 3 4 5 6 7 8 9

PRINTED IN THE UNITED STATES OF AMERICA

To All My Children

Contents

Introduction 1

CHAPTER I   A Whale of a Time 5
  1. Whale-watching   5

CHAPTER II   All Aboard! 13
  2. White Pass and Yukon Railway   13
  3. Agawa Canyon Excursion   15
  4. The Polar Bear Express   17
  5. The Hudson Bay   18

CHAPTER III   Down on the Farm 21
  6. Farm Holidays   21

CHAPTER IV   A Wilderness Adventure 26
  7. Outward Bound   26

CHAPTER V   The Offbeat Arctic 29
  8. Bathurst Inlet Lodge   29
  9. Arctic Overnighter   32
  10. Midnight Golf Tournament   34
  11. The Only Road to the Arctic   35

CHAPTER VI   The Spell of the Yukon 38
  12. The Robert Service Cabin   39
  13. Palace Grand   42
  14. Diamond Tooth Gertie's   43
  15. Panning for Gold   43
  16. The Chilkoot Trail   45

17. Kluane National Park 46
18. Dogsled Holiday 48

CHAPTER VII   Big-City Wonders 50
19. Fairview Cemetery, Halifax 50
20. Water Street, St. John's 51
21. Plains of Abraham, Quebec 52
22. World's Most Active Underground City 52
23. Kensington Market, Toronto 53
24. The Island, Toronto 53
25. Canada's Wonderland 54
26. Golden Boy, Winnipeg 55
27. Capilano Suspension Bridge, Vancouver 57
28. Grouse Mountain, Vancouver 58
29. Marine Museum, Victoria 58

CHAPTER VIII   Two Capital Ideas 60
30. The Noonday Gun 61
31. The National Aeronautical Collection 62

CHAPTER IX   Oddities Along the Trans-Canada 65
32. Ouimet Canyon 65
33. Kakabeka Falls 67
34. Carberry Desert 67
35. The Cypress Hills 68
36. Dinosaur Provincial Park 69
37. Hell's Gate 70
38. Saint-Jean Port Joli 71
39. The Kissing Bridge 72
40. Magnetic Hill 73
41. Alexander Graham Bell Museum 73
42. Woodleigh Replicas 74

CHAPTER X   Happy Trails 76
43. Trail Rides in the Rockies 76
44. Ontario Trail Rides 81
45. Hiking the Bruce Trail 82
46. The Pangnirtung Pass 84
47. White Water Rafting 85

48. Houseboat Holiday 88
49. The Ferry Cruise 90
50. Cruise Ships 92
51. Soaring Like an Eagle 93

CHAPTER XI Offbeat Accommodation 95
52. All the Comforts of Home 95
53. Canada's Left Bank 97
54. The Country Circuit 99
55. Newfie for a Day 100
56. On Campus 102
57. In Jail 102
58. Inexpensive Digs in the Rockies 103

CHAPTER XII Offbeat Dining 106
59. Lobster Suppers 106
60. Muck-a-Muck 108
61. A Taste of History 108
62. Top of the World 109

CHAPTER XIII Our Glorious Past 110
63. The Viking Settlement 110
64. Archaic Indians Burial Ground 112
65. Where North America Begins 113
66. Uncle Tom's Cabin 114
67. Norman Bethune Birthplace 116
68. Home of the Mennonites 117
69. Fortress Louisbourg 121
70. The World's Smallest Church 123
71. St. Boniface Cathedral 123
72. Christ Church Cathedral,
    the Haunted Church 124

CHAPTER XIV Natural Wonders 126
73. On Safari in Darkest Ontario 126
74. Flowerpot Islands 129
75. Queen Charlotte Islands 130
76. The Big Fishing Hole 131
77. The Unknown Spa 132
78. Bonaventure Island Seabird Sanctuary 134

79. Birdwatching on Grand Manan 135
80. Kouchibouguac National Park 136
81. Witless Bay Islands Seabird Sanctuary 136
82. Cape St. Mary's 137
83. Jack Miner Bird Sanctuary 137
84. Going Underground 139

CHAPTER XV Festivals and Other Special Events 141

85. Metro International Caravan 141
86. World Championship Bathtub Race 142
87. Quidi Vidi Lake Regatta 143
88. The Queen's Plate 143
89. The Canadian Club Classic 144
90. Shakespeare and Shaw 144
91. *The Trial of Louis Riel* 145
92. Old Time Fiddlers Contest 146
93. Calgary Stampede 147
94. Quebec Winter Carnival 148
95. Oktoberfest 149
96. The World's Biggest Annual Fall Fair 149

CHAPTER XVI Getting Around 152

97. Jet Holidays 152
98. Train Tours 153
99. Nature Tours 154
100. Young-Adult Adventures 155
101. An Exchange Bargain 156

Getting Around: Some General Information 156

Introduction

Ever dream of pitching a tent beside mountains loftier than the Alps?

Or going on safari among prides of lions that roam freely just outside your car?

Or rafting down a river with 2,000-foot cliffs rising on either side of you?

Or hopping on a horse and heading for secret places that are out of reach of the almighty automobile?

Or bobbing in a bay filled with playful whales?

Stop dreaming.

You don't have to seek out exotic lands half a world away to do any of the above. They are all waiting for you in Offbeat Canada. As is the spot where the Vikings landed in North America 500 years before Columbus. And the northern shack where some of Dangerous Dan McGrew's pals were born.

If these things don't sound much like the Canada you thought you knew, you're not alone. Most people think of this second largest land on earth as a place that's as comfortable, and as interesting, as an old pair of shoes.

OFFBEAT CANADA

Sure, it has mountains taller than any in Europe. Yes, its lakes do number in the millions and its forests in the tens of thousands of square miles. Indeed, its cities are now winning world-wide attention, with Montreal hosting both a world's fair and the Olympics within a single decade and prestigious *Fortune* magazine acclaiming Toronto as "the world's newest great city."

But the idea just won't go away that the face of Canada is as familiar as your sister's. No place to go seeking the exotic, the absurd, the weird or the wonderful. The worst aspect of this view of Canada is that it simply isn't so. There is an Offbeat Canada out there, one so varied that few countries on earth come close to matching its scope. This book is aimed at helping you discover it.

Some of the parts of Offbeat Canada we want to introduce you to are major discoveries, such as the fact that the biggest wild creatures the world has ever known are to be seen and photographed not on an African safari but in the bays of the island province of Newfoundland. Others are minor eccentricities such as a falls that runs uphill or a church that is still haunted by one of Florence Nightingale's nurses. But all of them will uncover for you a much more unconventional Canada than the one you thought you knew.

We will show you how to hole up for a day or two on Canada's Left Bank, take you down on the farm for a family holiday or just for an overnight stop as you cross the country. Along the way we'll take a gander at such things as a Grand Canyon no one knows about or a spot where you can go panning for gold in the Klondike.

But before you set off to make your fortune, let me introduce myself. My name is Gerry Hall; I am the travel editor of the Toronto *Star*, Canada's largest daily newspaper. I have made my way across Canada dozens of times in sixteen years as a travel writer, always on the lookout for unusual, and also affordable, vacation opportunities. In a single trip, I logged nearly 10,000 miles zigzagging my way from St. John's, Newfoundland, to Victoria, British Columbia.

I have found working ranches in the west that take in guests, even a former jailhouse in Ottawa that does. I have slept on houseboats bobbing on hideaway lakes and bunked in with a Newfoundland fishing family. I will take you to a golf tournament where they tee off at midnight and to a festival where you can experience food, drink and entertainment from among fifty ethnic groups all in the same week on a shoestring budget trip around the world.

In all, *Offbeat Canada* presents 101 vacation ideas, though these may well be just scratching the surface of the possibilities in a country that sprawls across 3,851,809 square miles and stretches north and south from the shadow of the North Pole to Pelee Island, on the same latitude as northern California, and east and west across seven time zones from the Atlantic to the Pacific.

Now, here we go, off to see a side of the Big Land most people miss completely.

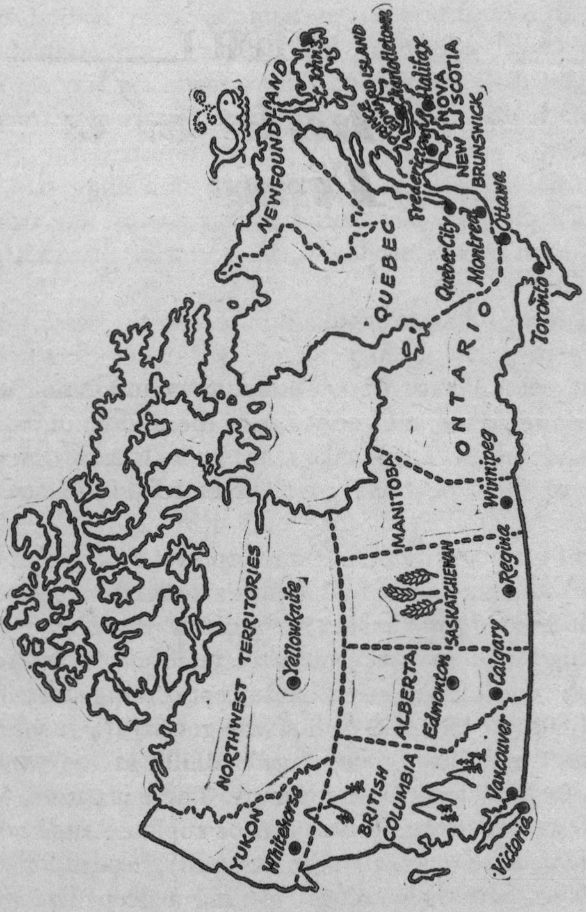
YUKON
Whitehorse
NORTHWEST TERRITORIES
Yellowknife
BRITISH COLUMBIA
Vancouver
Victoria
ALBERTA
Edmonton
Calgary
SASKATCHEWAN
Regina
MANITOBA
Winnipeg
ONTARIO
Toronto
Ottawa
QUEBEC
Quebec City
Montreal
NEWFOUNDLAND
St. John's
PRINCE EDWARD ISLAND
Charlottetown
Halifax
NOVA SCOTIA
NEW BRUNSWICK
Fredericton

CHAPTER I
A Whale of a Time

1. Whale-watching

When a whale dived a few feet away and passed under our fishing boat bobbing in the middle of Newfoundland's Placentia Bay, we quickly realized we were dealing with the largest creatures on the face of this earth.

We stared down into the clear waters of this bay on the south coast of Canada's rock-ribbed island province and saw him glide beneath us, almost close enough to touch. We couldn't believe how long it took him to make his pass. He kept coming and coming, till all 50 feet of him were gone. "It's just like *Jaws!*" cried fisherman Jim O'Reilly as the whale broke the surface 20 yards away. There it paused for a second or two as if waiting for applause and then, waving good-bye with his flukes (tail), headed for the depths. We knew he was making a deep dive this time because he created a minor whirlpool that, from where we were sitting, looked like something the *Titanic* might have left behind.

At that moment we knew for sure we were participating in one of the unusual travel adventures available in Canada. People travel halfway around the world to see big game in Africa without realizing that the biggest game of all is to be seen in the bays of Newfoundland. Whales are the largest creatures ever to inhabit the earth and are among the most interesting and mysterious. Humpback whales, such as the one we encountered, sing incredibly beautiful songs. And they call to each other over distances of more than a hundred miles. Moreover, as you will discover for yourself if you take part in this kind of adventure on a trip to Canada's east coast, it isn't so much a case of your going whale-watching as it is of the whale coming to watch you and perhaps having a bit of fun with the Lilliputian intruders he may find in his bay.

Whales have become a controversial subject in Newfoundland and there are even reports of fishermen carrying guns aboard their boats to shoot at them. For though it is well documented that whales are among the gentlest of all creatures, many Newfoundland fishermen either fear or hate them. Whales have a habit of getting entangled in fishing nets, especially the complex and expensive ones set out to catch cod. You can imagine what happens to these nets when a creature, weighing from 15 to 40 tons, thrashes around to get free. Some can't escape and drown, because as air-breathing mammals they can't make it to the surface; others are freed by Newfoundland whale-rescue groups while others free themselves or are killed by fishermen angered by this threat to their livelihood.

The situation has reached crisis proportions of late because more and more whales are invading the many bays around Newfoundland in search of the tiny capelin (a kind of ocean smelt) that supplies most of their diet. This invasion is intensified by the fact that several species of whale are returning from the edge of extinction because of bans on whale-hunting by countries such as Canada and reduced killing by other nations as a result of international pressure.

Whatever the cause, it's bad news for net fishermen but good news for whale-watchers. Some scientists believe that Newfoundland is now the whale-watching capital of the world. A major "whale contact" operation has been available on Trinity Bay for a couple of years now. Also, there are simply splendid opportunities to go whale-watching on your own. Which is what a friend and I did last summer.

We simply showed up in Long Harbour (80 miles or 130 kms west of St. John's) about 10 A.M. and asked whether there were any whales out in the bay. "They're thick enough that you could walk across the water on their backs," said one oilskin-clad fisherman, without looking up from the cod he was gutting. We asked if there might be a fisherman around who would take us out to see them and were steered to Jim O'Reilly, who worked for a year and a half in Toronto to help finance his own fishing boat.

"Yes, I spotted plenty of whale when I was out jiggin' for cod this morning," O'Reilly reported, "and I'll be glad to take you out." Well, the whales weren't quite thick enough to walk across but we spotted dozens of them blowing spray in the air among the islands that lie just off Long Harbour. Most of them stayed on the surface as we approached slowly, looked us over until we got within twenty yards or so and then did the deep dive that is characterized by the good-bye wave of the flukes you may be familiar with from commercial aquatic shows. But the one that dove under our boat stayed on the surface until we were a few feet from him. That's when O'Reilly mentioned that he had gone to see *Jaws* three times. We kind of wished he hadn't brought up the subject. On the way back to harbor three small whales or dolphins leaped just off our bow as if they were training for Marineland. The expedition cost us $15 each, though in truth O'Reilly was willing to settle for $10. He neither hates nor fears the whales he sees spouting off as he fishes each day—but then he catches his cod by jigging, not with nets.

O'Reilly did a splendid job of finding whales for us but for more serious whale-watchers there is a first-rate operation run by Peter Beamish, a biologist and acoustician who is known locally as "the whale man of Trinity Bay." Beamish walked away from a three-secretary government job in 1978 to "dedicate the rest of my life to increasing contact between whales and humans." His government job was to find out how whales used sonar to find food supplies. He ended up by establishing that they didn't use sonar at all for this purpose and in the course of his work "got completely hung-up on whales." He believes that Newfoundland is "the finest whale lab in the world" and sees whale-watching tourists as playing an important part in its development by establishing these deepsea jumbos as a key island attraction.

So he has set up shop in the historic little port of Trinity, 160 miles or 260 kms northwest of St. John's on Trinity Bay. Here hundreds of whales, who winter in the Caribbean and Bermuda, spend their summers. Beamish has bought the historic Village Inn in Trinity and turned it into a headquarters for what he calls "whale contact" expeditions. "You can't say whale-watching because they're watching us, too," he points out. In a few cases, this contact has been so close that participants have been able to reach out from inflatable boats and actually touch a whale. But even when that isn't possible, they do get close enough to observe the whales and watch their responses to the presence of humans. For example, Beamish is a musician and on occasion takes an accordion out with him. When he plays, whales sometimes stop to listen, moving on when the music ends.

Beamish believes that Newfoundland offers a better location for whale contact than more southerly destinations because the whales have finished calving when they head north and "aren't up-tight" about their young. Moreover, the concentration of whales in the Atlantic around Newfoundland may be the greatest in the world, with estimates by reputable experts running as high as 50,000.

Beamish offers intensive whale-watching adventures costing more than $1,200 for 12 days, and they sell out months in advance. Participants get to the whales by yacht and are lowered into rubber dinghies for close-ups. If whale sightings are scarce on Trinity Bay, Beamish is prepared to zip participants to other bays as soon as sightings are reported. He also has a trained staff of whale guides to accompany each outing.

If your interest in whales is more casual and you are planning a trip to Newfoundland and can get to Trinity on your own, there are 3-day expeditions offered costing about $200 and including 2 nights' accommodation, most meals, chartered yachts and guides.

If you have only a day to spare on a Newfoundland trip, it's still worth trying to contact Beamish (709-464-3269) the night before you hit the Trinity Bay area to see if he can arrange a fishing boat to take you out and send a guide along. Such a trip will cost you about $30 per person, depending on the size of your party.

Tourist visits are only a small part of the Beamish operation on Trinity Bay, which is aimed at producing meaningful communication between whales and man. He runs one of the whale hot-lines on the island, whose purpose is to free trapped whales without harming them. Since he can sometimes do so without great damage to nets, Beamish hopes fishermen will call him rather than kill a trapped whale. He also supplies underwater transmitters that can be attached to nets and fish traps in an attempt to ward off whales. Some of these transmit the cries of the feared killer whale but Beamish admits there is no proof that this cry will scare off some of the larger whales. In fact, there are still many things man doesn't know about the whale. His migratory paths aren't charted like those of the birds and no one has the slightest idea what whales do at night—except other whales, that is.

And, if you're still indifferent to whales, consider this: when a whale is trapped, his fellows appear to leave a "standby" whale around to look out for him. There is even evidence of whales getting under a sick member of the clan and pushing him to the surface so he can breathe. All of which takes a whale of a lot of caring.

The St. Lawrence River, especially around the spot where the Sanguenay River spills into it, also provides a marvelous whale-watching site in summer. Expeditions are led by Montreal zoologist Gerald Iles, who has made more than two dozen successful trips to see whales during the past ten years. Blue whales, belugas, humpbacks, fin, sei and minke are regularly spotted, and on one occasion, Iles estimates that people on his tour saw 300 to 400 belugas at one time.

Iles runs 2 types of trip. One is a 6-day affair in which passengers sail from Montreal on the new 88-foot motor ship Concordia, which offers an upper deck for close-ups of the whales and a cozy lounge below. There is no sleeping accommodation aboard so those taking part in the tour stay at hotels along the way. Expect to pay about $360 for each of 2 sharing a room.

Iles also offers weekend trips, mostly in August, in which passengers are bused from Montreal to Rivière du Loup, where a lecture with slides is given on whales. After overnighting there, passengers board a boat at nearby Trois Pistoles to go whale hunting, returning to Montreal that evening. Cost of this trip, without meals, is about $130.

The Zoological Society of Montreal also runs similar St. Lawrence whale-watching expeditions.

CONTACT

To arrange Newfoundland whale-watching expeditions, write to Peter Beamish, Village Inn, Box 10, Trinity, Trinity Bay, Newfoundland A0C 2S0.

For the St. Lawrence, contact Gerald Iles, 2053 Vendome Ave., Montreal, Quebec H4A 3M4, or Zoological Society of Montreal, 2055 Peel St., Montreal, Quebec, H3A 1V4.

CHAPTER II
All Aboard!

North American trains may seem in danger of becoming as extinct as North Atlantic ocean liners but they are still a great way to see Canada. There are transcontinental trains that offer a picture window on the Rockies and sleek turbo trains that zip between Toronto and Montreal in just 4 hours. But even these don't make our list of the great adventure trains still left for you to ride. When the conductor cries, "All aboard," we would suggest you be on one of the following: the narrow-gauge White Pass and Yukon Railway, the Algoma Central Railway's Agawa Canyon excursion, the Polar Bear Express or the Hudson Bay run from Winnipeg to Churchill on the shores of Hudson Bay.

2. White Pass and Yukon Railway

If we had to pick just one, we would ride the White Pass and Yukon Railway and leave the others for another year. It is probably the No. 1 rail adventure left on this continent; it follows the Klondike Gold Rush Trail of '98 through Canada's loftiest mountains from Skagway, Alaska, to Whitehorse in the Yukon.

This scenic wonder of a railway, just 110 miles in all, was conceived at the height of the gold rush as a supply line to the mine fields that had captured the imagination of the world. Sourdoughs, "clean mad for that muck called gold," as poet Robert Service said, were clawing their way up mountains through the same White Pass that today's train follows when the railway was begun. When you ride the cars of this turn-of-the-century narrow-gauge railway, one of the last remaining in North America, you can't help but be awestruck by the realization that work crews using pick and shovel were able to carve it up a 3,000-foot-high pass booby-trapped with avalanches and ice fields, sheer cliffs and roaring rivers. And you wonder, too, at how well this railway has withstood the ravages of time and the elements amid snow-capped peaks that seem designed as a backdrop for it alone. Beside you for part of the journey is the old White Pass trail, worn smooth in solid rock by thousands of gold-crazed sourdoughs.

The White Pass Railway was built mostly to handle freight—and that is still its main job. But it has become famous enough for its scenery and the chance it affords to ride back in time to one of the world's most riotous moments so that its passenger cars do a fine business in summer despite its remote location. It is especially popular with Alaska-bound cruise-line passengers docking at Skagway. In fact, many of them consider it the highlight of their whole voyage.

The White Pass can be ridden from either Whitehorse or Skagway or from either town to midway Bennett and back. But keep in mind that the most glorious scenery lies along the Bennett-Skagway portion which drops through a mountain valley that will leave you breathless by the mile.

CONTACT

For information, write to the White Pass and Yukon Railway, P.O. Box 435, Skagway, Alaska 99840, or the Ministry of Tourism, Box 2703, Whitehorse, Yukon Y1A 2C6.

3. Agawa Canyon Excursion

The Algoma Central Railway's Agawa Canyon Excursion takes you into the most awesome piece of scenery east of the Rockies. The canyon is off by itself in the middle of nowhere, 114 miles north of Sault Ste. Marie. You can't reach it by car, boat or plane. Only the snaking tracks of the Algoma Central cut through the endless Agawa forests where bears and wolves greatly outnumber people.

The excursion into the middle of the canyon takes most of the day, leaving the Soo (as Sault Ste. Marie is always known in the north) at 8 A.M. and returning that evening. The first 2 hours of the trip may leave you wondering if you somehow got on the wrong train—plenty of trees, just as they said, but nothing else at all. Then, it's as if Casey Jones takes over at the throttle and things start happening. You find yourself slicing between rock cuts only 50 feet apart and sift across one trestle over the Montreal River that is 1,550 feet long and 130 feet above the water. Lake after lake comes right to the edge of the tracks.

The train climbs slowly to a height of 1,600 feet then plunges suddenly more than 500 feet in just a 12-mile span to the floor of the canyon, where you can get off for 2 hours of picnicking and gawking. On every side of you, sheer cliffs climb into the skies. Some are forested right to the top while others show the bare precambrian rock that makes this part of the north so rugged. The Agawa River meanders through the middle of the canyon and a park with picnic tables has been set up on both sides, with plenty of cool green places to lie back and take in the show.

Short walks will take you to 2 waterfalls higher than Niagara. At Black Beaver Falls you can climb large rocks into the middle of the cascading water. The other, Bridle Vale, looks like lace curtains as it plunges several hundred feet to the river. A viewing tower lets you take in the whole canyon at one gasp—but be forewarned, there are lots of gasps on the way up, more than 300 steps to the top. If you are a fisherman, take your rod along on the train. Several prized speckled trout holes are found on the canyon section of the river.

By the way, most of the 100,000 people who pack the Agawa trains come in midsummer. But the canyon is at its best in autumn when its walls are ablaze in scarlet and gold. Daily trips leave the Algoma Central's downtown Soo depot, just off the Trans-Canada Highway, from late May until mid October. You can't make advance reservations but you can buy tickets a day ahead once you arrive in the Soo. Fare is $19.

If you are seeking an even more offbeat adventure, the Algoma Central runs its tourist snow train along the same tracks from January to March.

CONTACT
Algoma Central Railway, Box 7000, Sault Ste. Marie, Ontario P6A 5P6. But remember, no reservations can be made by mail.

4. The Polar Bear Express

The Polar Bear Express runs from the northern Ontario lumber town of Cochrane to Moosonee on the tidewaters of James Bay through forests not yet penetrated by even the faintest excuse for a road. Thus, the Ontario Northland Railway's Polar Bear Express has always been a lifeline to this remote corner of Ontario.

Once, the term Polar Bear Express was just a joke. For, true to its role, the train stopped for anyone who flagged it down. It carried a colorful assortment of trappers, hunters, prospectors, canoeists, local Indians and fishermen. And it still does. But now most tourists ride the real express along the same line, one that can take them on a day trip down to Arctic tidewaters and get them back to "civilization" that same day. The tourist train runs from July until Labor Day, daily except Friday. If you have time to take the slow train, make sure you have overnight reservations in Moosonee, a former Hudson's Bay

Company trading post founded in 1673, because digs are more than just scarce there with only 2 small lodges from which to choose. Keep in mind that the nearest road to anywhere else lies 150 miles to the south.

Most visitors to Moosonee take a 15-minute boat ride over to Moose Factory Island, site of the original trading post, where a blacksmith's shop is among eighteenth-century buildings that remain. There is a small museum there devoted to early fur-trade days. A freighter canoe can also take you to Fossil Island where formations are from the Devonian Age of 350 million years ago. Also take a peek in St. Thomas Church where the altar cloth is made of moosehide and prayer books are in the Cree language. You may find the overall appearance of Moosonee, with its clapboard shacks, disappointing. But you will leave knowing full well you have experienced a slice of northern outpost life the way it really is. Roundtrip fare is about $20.

CONTACT
Ontario Northland Railway, 805 Bay St., Toronto, Ontario M5S 1Y9.

5. The Hudson Bay

The sight of polar bears in the wild is the thing that makes The Hudson Bay a train to capture the imagination. It makes the run from Winnipeg to Churchill, the sub-Arctic port on Hudson Bay, both summer and winter. If you are hardy enough to make the run in winter you will likely find polar bears roaming the streets of Churchill. You can count on seeing some of them simply by taking a ride down to the town dump, a favorite foraging haunt for these mighty white denizens of the north.

The Hudson Bay makes the 500-mile run from Winnipeg to Churchill 3 times a week, departing Sunday, Tuesday and Thursday. You are sure of meeting a colorful cast of northern trappers, hunters and miners aboard because train and plane are the only ways of crossing the frozen muskeg to the shores of Hudson Bay. In fact, the northern section of the track bed of this unique rail line has been insulated so it won't damage the muskeg by causing it to melt. The result is that the line floats on top, causing trains to rock gently as they roll along. Don't expect an express run to the edge of the Arctic, however. The Hudson Bay makes 3 stops en route of more than an hour and a half each and takes a day and 2 nights in either direction. However, it reaches Churchill in the morning and doesn't depart until supper which gives you enough time to see the sights.

If you decide to stay over, you have 4 hostelries to choose from—the Arctic Inn, Tundra, Polar and Beluga Whale. Churchill is a busy grain port in summer but since Hudson Bay is frozen over for 8 months of the year, it is a fairly quiet place in winter—except for polar bears. It is estimated that 12,000 of the world's 20,000 polar bears live in Canada and their largest denning ground is just 30 miles south of town. These bears are so dangerous that it is suggested visitors go to the local RCMP office on arrival to get instructions on what to do if they run into one of these white, 1,000-pound giants. The real trick is to avoid them, or to make sure you see them from the inside of a bus or car. If that isn't possible, the best bet is to lie down and play dead. Outrunning them is impossible; even with their great bulk they can do 20 miles an hour and take a man's head off with one mighty swipe of their paws.

On a gentler note, whales are often sighted just off shore by summer visitors. And you can visit the 200-year-old ruins of Fort Prince of Wales, which despite its 14-foot walls fell to the French in 1782 without a shot being fired.

The Hudson Bay is operated by VIA, the government agency that runs most passenger trains in the country. It is equipped with coaches, sleepers and dining cars, with one-way fare in the $60 range.

CONTACT
Bookings can be made through VIA Rail Canada Inc., 20 King St. W., 5th floor, Toronto, Ontario M5H 1C4. In the U.S., Amtrak will make bookings on VIA trains.

CHAPTER III
Down on the Farm

6. Farm Holidays

The little boy from the city wasn't all that surprised when the bull started talking to him. When you are six, you tend to take talking bulls for granted. But his parents needed an explanation for the talking bull of North River, Prince Edward Island, and farmer Ron MacKinley finally agreed to give them one. Ron had put a walkie-talkie near the bull and then hidden himself in a loft above. When the little boy approached the stall and the bull said "hello," the two were soon engrossed in deep conversation with the bull telling the little boy all about his life down on the farm and the boy telling him what he did for fun in the city.

That kind of homespun fun is the essence of a Canadian farm holiday, an offbeat vacation that is now available in every Canadian province except Newfoundland. From Atlantic to Pacific, farm organizations are now ready to put city slickers in contact with country cousins willing to put them up for a week or 2 at rates which are usually about half what a hotel would charge.

It could be a cattle ranch in Alberta, a wheat farm in Saskatchewan, a fruit farm in Ontario or a potato patch in Prince Edward Island or New Brunswick. Some offer a trout stream running through the place; others are just minutes from an ocean beach. Some offer horses to ride and others welcome a guest who wants to try his hand at milking a cow or helping with the chores.

But no matter how they differ, all offer an escape from city cares into a world where you can still hear the birds by day and the frogs by night, a world that smells of new-mown hay and fresh apple pies, a world where tractors may have replaced horses but not the horse-and-buggy pace of life. Forget about nightlife, there won't be any except for the occasional euchre game or a square dance in the local community center. But expect days that will leave you so pleasantly ready for bed that you won't care.

You may spend your days just walking through the fields or exploring winding country roads in your car. Some farms offer such extras as riding horses, organized hayrides or a fishing pond right on the property. Several provincial organizations now produce booklets that describe the properties of each participating farm. Most farm families are willing to have guests help with the chores if they want and, of course, most farmers are more than willing to give you their side of the food-price squeeze story that seems to be bothering all of us these days. But you have to make some concessions, too, to the fact that most farm families wake with the dawn to get a jump on the day's work. You are usually given your own key or simply told, "Oh, we never lock the door so come and go when you please." Take them at their word, but make sure you do it quietly if it's later than 11 P.M. when you arrive back at the spread.

Home-cooked food is one of the highlights of a farm vacation and this is one area in which few country families let you down. Breakfast usually includes farm-fresh eggs and cream, even bacon from pigs raised by the farmer himself. Toast or freshly baked biscuits just keep coming until you have had your fill. Not all farm families are prepared to supply 3 meals a day, but some also offer guests supper that will usually include a roast and vegetables and salads right from the garden. We know one farmwife who always puts the water on to boil before she goes out to pick the corn. "It's the only way to make sure you don't lose any of the flavor," she insists. Many farm families still preserve their own fruit for desserts—they call it canning despite the fact that jars are always used. So expect a jar of preserved jam or pears to be part of most meals, too. You can still expect meals to begin with the saying of grace at many farms.

But don't expect modern luxury; you're not staying at a motel. In fact many of the farms taking part in holiday programs have been in the same family for more than a century. Air-conditioning will most likely consist of an open window catching the fresh night air.

Rates vary from farm to farm and from province to province, though some farm associations set a maximum daily charge. We paid $15 per adult and $9 per child, including breakfast, at the last farm we visited. When writing away to a prospective farm, besides inquiring about such things as riding horses, nearby swimming or entertainment facilities, it's also worth mentioning whether or not you drink or smoke. Some farm families just won't permit such city vices.

A farm holiday can be an exciting learning experience for your children in an age when some cities are considering putting horses in their zoos because they are so rarely seen by city youngsters. Down on the farm, the birds and bees are there for the seeing and so are newly born calves and piglets.

CONTACT

Remember that farm or organizations are usually small and informal and run by members on a voluntary basis. The current addresses are listed below. If they change, chances are good that your letter will be forwarded to the proper address.

Nova Scotia: Jack Hicks, Department of Agriculture, Extension Services Branch, Box 89, St. Peter's, Richmond County, Nova Scotia B0E 3B0.

New Brunswick Farm Vacation Association, Box 6000, Fredericton, New Brunswick E3B 5H1.

Prince Edward Island: Mrs. Florence Matheson, Oyster Bed Bridge, Winsloe, R.R.2, Prince Edward Island C0A 2H0.

Quebec: Federation des Agricultures de Quebec, 515 Avenue Viger, Montreal, Quebec H2L 2P2.

Ontario Vacation Farm Association, R.R.2, Erin, Ontario N0B 1T0.

Manitoba Farm Vacations Association, 437 Assiniboine Ave., Winnipeg, Manitoba R3C 0Y5.
Saskatchewan: Mrs. M. Moldenhauer, Box 214, Allan, Saskatchewan S0K 0C0.
Alberta: Mrs. Georgina Taylor, R.R. 1, Chuvin, Alberta T0B 0V0.
British Columbia: Farm Vacation Program, Ministry of Agriculture, Parliament Buildings, Victoria, British Columbia V8W 2Z7.

CHAPTER IV

A Wilderness Adventure

7. Outward Bound

Want a terrific idea for a novel New Year's Eve? How about spending it all by yourself in the middle of a frigid wilderness that could drop to 40 below. That's one of the many possibilities offered on an Outward Bound adventure. But before you go, be clear on one thing: Outward Bound does not offer holidays; it offers outdoor experiences designed to make you aware of your own abilities. Some people call them survival courses, but that's actually an oversimplification.

Outward Bound was born in Wales in 1941 and is the brainchild of Kurt Hahn. Its wartime purpose was to get merchant seamen physically and mentally ready to survive in case their vessel were sunk. The mental and emotional facets were given great emphasis in the program after it was noted that older seamen appeared to be able to survive in lifeboats while younger, apparently fit ones perished because they lacked the will to survive.

A Wilderness Adventure

In Canada, Outward Bound has its wilderness school at Black Sturgeon Lake, 90 miles north of Thunder Bay and 37 miles by gravel road from the Trans-Canada Highway at Hurkett. Here, participants pay from $425 to $1,225 to learn survival and other skills such as mushing through the bush on a dogsled, rock climbing, white-water canoeing, building a proper wood fire and staying warm sleeping outdoors when temperatures plunge. Courses lasting 10 to 35 days are offered at the school both winter and summer and are open to people from 15 years and up. A 67-year-old man recently came through the most difficult of all the courses with flying colors. Unfortunately, a 14-year-old Toronto boy drowned at the wilderness school in 1979. He was a nonswimmer. People applying to take an Outward Bound course must fill in a detailed medical report which also calls on their doctors to certify that they are in good enough shape to tackle the wilderness.

The key moment in most of the courses offered is when the participant does his solo, that is when he is left to fend for himself in the wilderness. In these cases, he is always within shouting distance of other soloists, but the idea is to survive on your own using the skills you have acquired. On a 21-day trip, for example, participants are expected to make it on their own for a 3-day period and travel the last 5 days of a wilderness canoe trip without the direct supervision of guides. Another program calls for a 6-mile paddle across an arm of Black Sturgeon Lake, a 1-mile portage, a 1-mile orienteering trip by compass through virgin forest and a 6-mile run back to camp.

No place for softies, to be sure, yet Outward

Bound also runs courses for office-bound business executives aimed at teaching them in the outdoors the necessity of working as a team, not as a group of individuals. Wilderness skills are taught, of course, but the emphasis is on getting along with other people, watching out for your fellow, learning to handle the stresses of group living. Outward Bound also runs a rock-climbing camp near Keremeos in British Columbia. The Canadian operation is part of a world-wide nonprofit organization with 30 schools in various countries.

CONTACT
For details on all courses offered, contact Outward Bound Wilderness School, Suite 200, 11 Yorkville Ave., Toronto, Ontario M4W 1L3.

CHAPTER V

The Offbeat Arctic

8. Bathurst Inlet Lodge

Mountie Glenn Warner was mushing his dogsled team through the Arctic snows when he came on a site that was to become one of Canada's most unusual tourist attractions. It was an abandoned Hudson's Bay Company trading post on Bathurst Inlet, lying inside the Arctic Circle in the distant reaches of the Northwest Territories. It was just another stop on Warner's RCMP beat but soon he began dreaming of turning it into a lodge that would introduce others to the Arctic he had come to love. One day he quit dreaming and bought the place. In 1969, after he retired from the force, he and his wife Trish opened for business.

What they offer is a chance to see the most magnificent wildlife this side of East Africa. The caribou herd on Bathurst Inlet alone is estimated at 250,000. "Of course, you can't see them all at once. But you are almost guaranteed to see a herd of a thousand or so," Warner says. The lodge also offers a chance to see and photograph arctic wolves, grizzly bear, musk ox, fox, lemmings and seals, along with 50 varieties of bird life, that include eagles, yellow-billed loons, hawks and owls. But no hunters need apply. This lodge is for nature lovers only and, though guests are welcome to do a spot of fishing, the Warners aren't interested in you if that's your prime concern. "We want to use all our facilities for the person who comes to enjoy nature," Warner says. Prince Charles was one of these.

The lodge is situated on the Burnside River where caribou migration trails are located. It can take more than a day for some of the herds to pass. Nearby, there are 3 scenic waterfalls and cataracts that plunge more than 100 feet. Visitors can see ancient Eskimo camps and burial grounds and the nesting areas of golden eagles and peregrine falcons. Trips are taken by boat to the Quadjuk Islands where sheer cliffs climb into the blue Arctic sky. Despite its remoteness—360 miles north of Yellowknife, the capital of the Territories—Warner hopes to see a national park established on Bathurst Inlet some day. For though it is the wildlife that attracts most visitors, this is also a region of extraordinary flora. Rather than the barren wastes most people expect, there is a tundra ablaze with roses, orchids and orange lichen, all set amid a sea of grass and small shrubs. "Once you've seen the place," says Warner, "you think of it almost every day. It changes your whole life."

His Bathurst Inlet Lodge may have the shortest season of any in Canada, running from mid June to the first week of September. But people who book in for a week have plenty of time for sightseeing as this is truly the Land of the Midnight Sun. In July, you can read a magazine or book outdoors at 2 A.M. Rates at the lodge may sound like those charged for an African Safari, though they are actually considerably less. The Warners get $1,575 a week all inclusive. That means you are picked up and then brought back to Yellowknife by plane after a week in which all meals, drinks, guide fees, use of boats and all other facilities have been included in the price. The guides, by the way, are native people who live by hunting and trapping most of the year. Eskimo carvings and other crafts are sold by their families to supplement their living.

Summer temperatures here and in the rest of the Northwest Territories are much higher than people expect. Days are often warm enough for swimming down around Yellowknife and even at Bathurst Inlet the mean temperature in summer is about 50 degrees, with some July days managing to squeak into the 80s Fahrenheit. This treeless frontier gives a visitor the impression that he is in a vast wilderness and the figures certainly back up that first impression. The Northwest Territories are larger than Alaska, Texas, California and New Mexico put together, sprawling across 1,304,903 square miles (3,376,698 sq. km.) With a population of only 50,000 there are nearly 30 square miles for each man, woman and child.

Although you won't get to see them, the Territories are the home of one of the world's most glamorous endangered species. All the 50-odd whooping cranes left in the wild were born in Wood Buffalo

National Park on the border between the Territories and Alberta. Although you can drive in to see the park's buffalo herd, the whooping cranes hatch their young in a remote corner of the park, far away from the enemy called man who has all but eradicated a species that once numbered in the millions.

CONTACT
For Bathurst Inlet Lodge, write to Bathurst Inlet Developments Ltd., Box 820, Yellowknife, Northwest Territories X0E 1H0.
For a first-rate free guide to the entire Northwest Territories, write to TravelArctic, Yellowknife, Northwest Territories X1A 2L9 and ask for a copy of the *Explorers' Guide to Canada's Arctic*. Because tourist facilities and towns are so limited in the Territories, this government guide is able to outline them all.

9. Arctic Overnighter

An early-morning conversation in a Toronto office: "Gee, you look done in. Where were you last night?"

"Up in the Arctic visiting some Eskimos."

Ridiculous as it may seem, an answer like that can be the gospel truth. Thousands of sightseers take overnight trips from both Toronto and Montreal to Frobisher Bay on Baffin Island from early June to early August. Frobisher, the largest airport in Canada's far north, lies just outside the Arctic Circle, but the plane makes a loop into the Arctic before landing in this gateway to the eastern Arctic. Planes leave Toronto and Montreal at 7 P.M. and get you back to town in time for work the next morning. Yet Frobisher is farther north of the southern extremities of Canada than Cuba is south of them. What makes an Arctic overnighter possible is that this part of the world is the Land of the Midnight Sun in early summer. When you land at Frobisher, you can expect the town's children to be at the airport to meet you, hoping for a handout and a glimpse of the funny southerners who would fly so far to see something that is so commonplace to them. Restaurants and craft shops stay open and three school buses, the only buses on Baffin Island, wait to take you on a tour for part of the 5½ hours you have to see the true north.

When you enter the restaurant for a snack, you get an idea of the harsh realities of life in a community where all the food must be flown in. Coffee is 60 cents, a hotdog $1.35, a small steak and french fries are $10. Householders pay $3.50 for 2 pounds of apples and 40 cents for a liter of gasoline. When you tour the sleeping town, you learn that a 2-bedroom apartment rents for as much as $730. Some people on the tour come expecting to find igloos. They are disappointed at the prefabs that house this community of 2,500. Some find the surroundings bleak—treeless, rocky hills that are only occasionally covered with bright Arctic flowers and lichen. Unfortunately, some of the most interesting buildings in town are closed to the night visitors, such as the igloo-shaped Anglican church with its cross of narwhal tusks and Inuit wall decorations. But your guided tour takes you out of town to see the DEW Line installations, built by the U.S. and turned over to Canada in 1963, and TV installations that bring 3 stations and what we call civilization to the Inuit people whose ancestors came to the isolation of the Arctic 5,000 years ago. The bus tour also takes you to a small museum of Inuit art and to a shop where you can buy soapstone carvings and other Eskimo handicrafts before returning to the airport. There you can purchase other handicrafts and frozen Arctic char before boarding a 737 jet for the flight home. This trip is not a northern feast by any means but a small taste that leaves some visitors longing for more.

The return flight costs about $280, including airport taxes, but still manages to all but sell out for the whole season.

CONTACT
Goliger's Tours, 188 University Ave., Suite 415, Toronto, Ontario M5H 3C3 can supply details on departure dates for 1981.

10. Midnight Golf Tournament

Yellowknife, while north of the 60th parallel, is well outside the Arctic Circle, which lies some 300 miles to the north. But we are including its oddball sports event in this section because Yellowknife is the capital of Canada's Arctic. In mid June, it holds the Annual Midnight Golf Tournament with players teeing off from 12 A.M. onward. Don't expect manicured greens; they are oiled-down sand. But do expect a lot of fun in a tournament where there is no penalty if a raven steals your ball.

CONTACT
If you want to play, contact Harvard Budgeon, Yellowknife Inn, Box 490, Yellowknife, Northwest Territories X0E 1H0.

11. The Only Road to the Arctic

For the man who's been everywhere, there's still something almost no one has done—drive to the Arctic. After twenty years of construction, the $100 million Dempster Highway was finally opened in 1979 from near Dawson City in the Yukon to the edge of the Arctic Ocean at Inuvik in the Northwest Territories. It is Canada's only road to the Arctic.

Mind you, it's not for everyone. Only the daring, and preferably the daring with a four-wheel-drive vehicle or a car in excellent condition, need apply. For this is an often lonely gravel road winding for almost 500 miles over mountain and tundra. It takes from 15 to 18 hours to reach Inuvik on the edge of the Arctic Ocean once you leave the Alaska Highway, 25 miles southeast of Dawson. There's not an inch of pavement; it's gravel all the way. And the drive takes you through both the Ogilvie and Richardson mountain ranges. Once you take the fork in the road near Dawson, you won't spot another building for 230 miles until you arrive at the Eagle Plains Lodge where gasoline, a small repair shop, a trailer park, hotel and restaurant are lumped together in a complex that cost $3.5 million. From there, it is just over 100 miles to Fort McPherson in the Northwest Territories. Two river-ferry crossings at the Arctic Red River and Peel River must be made before you get to Inuvik.

As a reward for all that driving, you get to see the true north, treeless but populated by moose, grizzly bear, wolves, Arctic fox and great herds of caribou which migrate across the Dempster in fall and spring. Sometimes, in fact, traffic must be limited to avoid disturbing these great migrations. The road follows the route taken by Mountie William Dempster who set out from Dawson in 1911 in search of the famous Lost Patrol. Mushing across the tundra with a dog team, Dempster found all four members of the patrol dead. What made modern man take an interest in the route was not the tourist possibilities but oil exploration in the Beaufort sea which needed a land supply route.

By all means pack your fishing rod when you head out on the Dempster. Streams along the way are chock-full of trout and grayling. However, it is not a good idea to trust your fishing luck to feed you along the way; an adequate supply of food and a couple of extra spare tires are an excellent idea. Driving on gravel takes a bit of know-how. Keep car windows closed to minimize dust. If you don't have an air conditioner, open your vents and turn your controls to "defrost." Always slow down when meeting another car and don't accelerate excessively when passing one going your way. It's a good idea to fasten a rubber mat to the bottom of your gas tank to prevent stone damage and to attach a wire mesh to the front of your rad.

It's the sights along the way, the Arctic experience—not Inuvik itself—that makes the trip worthwhile. Despite its name, meaning "place of man," Inuvik is not an ancient Eskimo settlement but a modern town carved out of the wilderness in 1955. It is the main supply base for oil exploration in the area. Because of the special problems of building on permanently frozen ground, the town is a maze of above-ground steam, water and sewage pipes connecting every building.

Although the new route may be kept open all year for trucks carrying supplies, it is snow-free for only a short period in the summer. Ferry service on the 2 river crossings operates only from mid June until early October. In winter, supply trucks traveling in convoy make the river crossings on ice bridges.

CONTACT

If you are planning to drive the Dempster, it is worth contacting both the Yukon and Northwest Territories governments for maps and other details on road conditions. In the Territories, there is a toll-free number, Zenith 2022, that will give you the schedule for the 2 ferry crossings.

For the Northwest Territories, write to Travel-Arctic, Yellowknife, Northwest Territories X1A 2L9.

For the Yukon, the address is Yukon Department of Tourism, Box 2703, Whitehorse, Yukon Y1A 2C6.

CHAPTER VI

The Spell of the Yukon

"The great, big, broad land, 'way up yonder" that poet Robert Service unveiled to the world is still a special place for anyone in search of offbeat adventure. On a trip to the Yukon, you can find the cabin where Jack London answered *The Call of the Wild* and the one where Service fell under *The Spell of the Yukon*. You can even wander along "the marge of Lake Lebarge" where he cremated Sam McGee. In a land still permeated by the romance of its Klondike days, you can go panning for gold on Bonanza Creek, where the original strike was made, or ogle the dancehall girls at the Palace Grand, which had its heyday in 1899 when saloon janitors made small fortunes from the gold they found in the sweepings from the floor around the bar. You can try your luck at Diamond Tooth Gertie's, the only legalized Vegas-style gambling casino in all of Canada, or even follow the footsteps of the thousands of sourdoughs, "clean mad for the muck called gold," up the Chilkoot Trail on guided hikes.

But more than that, you can discover for yourself

what Service meant when he wrote "Listen to the wild—it's calling you" amid Canada's highest peaks in Kluane National Park. This largest of Canada's national parks preserves such a spectacular piece of scenery that it was declared a treasure of world-wide importance in 1980 when the United Nations added it to its list of World Heritage Sites.

The park and other attractions can now be reached over an impressive network of highways that criss-crosses the southern section of this 207,000-square-mile territory in the northwest corner of the country. The highways aren't all paved—in fact only a few miles are—but they are well maintained and should give the careful summer visitor no major problem. They also open the Yukon to mountain climbers, canoeists, rafters and hikers. But before you hit the road, there's one thing you should know. Natives don't call it "the Yukon" any more than people living to the south would call it "the Ontario," "the New York" or "the Alberta." North of the 60th parallel, it's just plain Yukon.

12. The Robert Service Cabin

Robert Service, whose poetry captured the essence of the Yukon for native and visitor alike, loved the two-room log cabin in Dawson where he lived from 1909 until 1912. He wrote a poem to it called "Goodbye, Little Cabin," part of which went this way:

> I've seen when you've been the best friend that I had

Your light like a gem on the snow;
You're sort of a part of me—Gee! but I'm sad;
I hate, little cabin, to go.

Service was already quite famous as the "Bard of the Yukon" when he lived in his cabin on the east side of Dawson, right in the center of the Klondike gold-strike area. Born in Preston, England, in 1874, he grew up in Scotland and emigrated to Canada in 1896, where he worked as a ranch hand and bookkeeper and farmer before getting a job as a clerk with the Bank of Commerce. Fate took over in 1904 when the bank transferred him to Whitehorse, now the capital of the Yukon but then just a small community at the terminus of the railway supply line from Skagway, Alaska.

He began tramping the woods, canoeing the rivers and lakes and listening to the tales of the sourdoughs. A friend suggested he write a poem "about our own bit of earth" to recite at a social evening. The sounds from the bars on a Saturday night put the words "A bunch of the boys were whooping it up" into his mind and he headed off to the quiet of the teller's cage in the bank to work on his poem. But he had forgotten about the night guard who, startled, drew his revolver and fired, missing him by inches. With thoughts of that bullet whizzing past his head and his first line already written, he created "The Shooting of Dan McGrew." Dozens of rhymes followed during the next few months. The first publisher Service sent them to was so elated that he promised an unheard of 10-percent royalty. Service's output got an additional spur when the bank transferred him to Dawson, once the "Paris of the North." He wrote *Ballads of a Cheechako* there and was soon receiving a handsome income of $5,000 a year from his books, enough to allow him to quit the bank and rent a cabin of his own in which to work. "Everything was snug and shipshape," he said. "I would not have exchanged my cabin for the palace of a king."

But in 1912 he did leave it and the Yukon forever, living mainly in France until his death in 1958. While occupying the cabin, however, he wrote a novel, *The Trail of Ninety-eight,* and a volume of poems, *Rhymes of a Rolling Stone.* Much of the material for both was garnered at a nearby cafe where Service used to sit down for lunch with a ramshackle group of sourdoughs. He later recalled his work in the cabin:

> I used to write on coarse rolls of paper . . . pinning them on the wall and printing my verses in big charcoal letters. Then I would pace back and forth before them, studying them, repeating them, trying to make them perfect.
>
> I tried to avoid my literary quality. Verse, not poetry, is what I was after. Something the man in the street would take notice of and the sweet old lady would paste in her album, something the schoolboy would spout and the fellow in a pub would quote.

Robert Service's cabin may well be the main literary shrine in all of Canada. Yukoners have looked on it that way almost from the start and have kept it intact; in 1970 it was turned over to Parks Canada as an historic site. You can tour the cabin and listen to recitations of Service's poetry at 4 P.M. daily.

The Yukon's other major literary figure, Jack London, spent a little less than a year in the Dawson area at the height of the gold rush. While in Dawson, he met a huge dog, whom he immortalized as "Buck" in *The Call of the Wild*, one of five books he wrote about the Yukon. *The Call of the Wild* still remains immensely popular the world over and has been published in 29 different languages, including Swahili. London, by the way, left the north after a bout of that bane of the sourdough— scurvy. A cabin used by London has been moved from nearby Henderson Creek to Dawson. Lectures and readings from his work are given there daily at 11 A.M.

13. Palace Grand

Though Dawson City is now almost a ghost town, with fewer than 1,000 permanent residents, it has done a fine job of preserving its famous and infamous past. At the height of the gold rush, Arizona Charlie Meadows built the Palace Grand as a combination dance hall and opera house, using lumber from two beached sternwheelers. The federal government restored it to its 1899 splendor and during the summer (May 30 to September 21) the Gaslight Follies, honkeytonk turn-of-the-century entertainment, is presented nightly except Monday.

14. Diamond Tooth Gertie's

Dawson is also the site of the only legalized gambling casino in Canada, Diamond Tooth Gertie's, where blackjack and roulette can be played Vegas-style. Gertie's has 3 floorshows nightly during its season which runs from the end of May until mid September. It is closed Sundays and Tuesdays and you must be at least 19 years old to enter.

The Dawson City Museum (admission $1) is filled with artifacts from gold-rush days. The city's 1901 post office has been restored to its Victorian splendor. Dawson lies along the Klondike Highway which connects with the Yukon's main artery, the Alaska Highway, at Whitehorse, 333 miles to the south. Despite it's small size, Dawson has 3 hotels, 9 motels and 4 restaurants. Expect to pay about $35 for a room.

15. Panning for Gold

Yes, thar's still gold in them thar' creeks. Several million dollars' worth is found each year, mostly by commercial operations; but a small percentage is found by visitors hunkered down at the edge of a stream panning for gold. Don't expect to get rich but do expect to have some fun trying your hand at it. All you need is a pan and a shovel. You can buy a prospector's pan at any hardware store in the Yukon but there's no need to go even to that expense if you have a pie pan 12 to 15 inches across and about 2 inches deep. It will do just fine. When you reach the stream where you want to work, get a small shovelful from a sand or gravel bar or from a pit in the stream bed itself. Dump it in your pie plate and you are ready to pan.

Panning works on the principle that gold, one of the heavier elements, will sink to the bottom of the pan with other heavy deposits while lighter materials will float to the top to be washed away. Put your pan just below the surface of the stream, first working through the contents to remove worthless pebbles and breaking up lumps of sand. Then you begin rotating the pan, shaking it gently under the water so lighter particles float away while the heavy stuff, containing, you hope, shiny, golden specks, sinks to the bottom of the pan. When you have removed most of the light material this way, carefully pour off most of the water and bounce the pan gently, as if you were flipping a flapjack, to spread the heavy sand across the bottom. Then your search starts in earnest, using a magnifying glass, if you've brought one along. Remember, with gold in the Yukon, it's finders keepers.

To find the right kind of stream, it is best to ask around Dawson first. After all, it was on nearby Rabbit Creek that George Carmack, Shookum Jim and Tagish Charlie made the August 17, 1896, strike that was heard around the world. Carmack immediately renamed the creek "Bonanza" and staked the first four claims. Though most who followed found misery instead of instant wealth, it is estimated that prospectors took $500 million in gold—at yesteryear's prices—from Yukon rivers, streams and hillsides, though the source or mother lode, if there was one, was never found. A cairn on Bonanza Creek marks the site of the find that started the stampede. Just above the cairn, the Klondike Visitors Association has its own claim where visitors can pan to their heart's content for free. But don't forget that a couple of hundred thousand other hopefuls have been there before you. Poverty Bar, also on Bonanza Creek, is a commercial panning operation.

16. The Chilkoot Trail

There is no more romantic trail in the world than the one the sourdoughs clawed their way up in 1898 from Skagway, Alaska, into the Yukon. You can follow in their footsteps on a rugged, 7-day guided hiking adventure through some of Canada's most dramatic mountain scenery. Hikers meet in Whitehorse, the capital of the Yukon, and are taken by mini-bus to Skagway. Guides, food, drink and first-aid supplies are included in the $500 price, as is hotel accommodation for the days of your arrival in and departure from Whitehorse. You have to bring along your own backpack and sleeping bag or rent one after your arrival.

CONTACT
Goldrush River Tours, Box 4835, Whitehorse, Yukon Y1A 2S3 will supply departure dates for these July and August hiking adventures. The Chilkoot, however, is just one of many hiking trails blazed by prospectors, trappers and Indians throughout the Yukon. You may obtain topographical maps by writ-

ing to the Resident Geologist, Room 103, Federal Building, Whitehorse, Yukon. June, July and August are the best hiking months.

17. Kluane National Park

When Yukon's 8,500-square-mile Kluane National Park was proclaimed a World Heritage Site by the United Nations in 1980, it joined such famed preserves as the Galápagos and the Everglades as places of special significance to the world. Yet few Canadians have ever laid eyes on this spectacular park, which can be reached in a 2-hour drive along the Alaska Highway from Whitehorse.

One of the world's largest national parks, Kluane contains 2 towering mountain ranges including Canada's highest peak, Mt. Logan (19,850 feet). The most massive ice fields outside the polar regions, wild rivers and a glamorous array of wildlife fill the spaces between the peaks. Kluane's massive glaciers are something special for the visitor, who is able to see clearly that they are the rivers of ice scientists tell us they are. Steele Glacier in the park was nicknamed "the galloping glacier" after having moved 7-miles in just 4 months during the 1960s. Kluane's animal population contains the largest concentration of dall sheep in the world, some 4,000, plus grizzlies, black bear, wolves and wolverines. The 180 kinds of birds spotted in the park include bald eagles, trumpeter swans and the virtually extinct peregrine falcon. Its rivers leap with Arctic grayling and kokanee salmon.

Headquarters for the park are located just off the

Alaska Highway, at mile 1019, north of Haines Junction. Here you can get information on the 11 hiking trails in the park, most of which follow old mining trails. Some of them are easy enough for an inexperienced hiker but anyone planning to enter Kluane's wilderness on an overnight trip—or one of longer duration—must register at park headquarters or at the information center at Sheep Mountain. There is only one campground in Kluane, located on Kathleen Lake, 15 miles south of Haines Junction. Mountain climbing has been a feature of Kluane ever since the Italian Duke of Abruzzi scaled Mt. St. Elias in 1897. During Canada's centennial, 250 climbers took part in an expedition up the Icefield or St. Elias range, which was said to be the largest ascent on a mountain since Hannibal crossed the Alps to attack Rome. Groups planning a climb in Kluane's big mountains must write for permission to the park superintendent three months in advance.

CONTACT
For information write to Superintendent, Kluane National Park, Mile 1019, Alaska Highway, Yukon Y0B 1L0.

Though the call of the wild is heard mainly by the outdoorsman, Yukon offers awesome scenery and offbeat adventure trips to less experienced visitors, too. There are guided river rafting trips, lasting for from 2½ hours to 2 weeks and costing from just $6 to nearly $600, that require no previous experience. Even some of the canoe trips are tailored for amateurs.

CONTACT

You can find out about specific trips as well as accommodation in the Yukon by writing to Tourism Yukon, Government of Yukon, Box 2703, Whitehorse, Yukon Y1A 2C6 and asking for the excellent *All About Yukon* book. Maps and brochures on various canoe, fishing, rafting and historic trips are also available free from the same source.

18. Dogsled Holiday

Tired of the usual holiday down south but looking for a way to get rid of the winter blahs? How about learning to mush a dogsled across a frozen British Columbia lake and staying in cabins along the way? Such a holiday is actually offered by Bruce Johnson at Atlin, British Columbia, on the Yukon border. Atlin is so remote that it is cut off completely from the rest of the province, the only connecting road coming in from Whitehorse in the Yukon, 110 miles to the north. You have to get yourself to Whitehorse where you are picked up and taken, partly by dogsled, to the Johnson cabin which is across frozen Atlin Lake from the town of Atlin. Then, for $125 a day, you are taught to drive a dogsled and to handle cross-country skiing in the far north. Applicants should be able to use cross-country skis and snowshoes.

CONTACT
Johnson's Sled Dogs, Box 14, Atlin, British Columbia V0W 1A0.

The Spell of the Yukon

CHAPTER VII

Big-City Wonders

Offbeat Canada isn't found only in remote parts of the country or along rarely traveled byways. Some of the country's weird and wonderful attractions are located in the heart of its major cities. Most of them are familiar to the natives but turn out to be major discoveries to the visitor who comes on them for the first time.

19. Fairview Cemetery, Halifax

In Halifax, you can visit Fairview Cemetery and discover the final chapter in the story of two of the worst sea disasters in the history of the world. In 1917 the collision of two ships, one loaded with munitions, in Halifax harbor touched off the biggest explosion to occur prior to World War II. Two thousand people died and one whole section of the city was flattened. A common monument in Fairview marks the spot where 249 unidentified victims were buried. Nearby, you will find rows of markers for victims of the sinking of the *Titanic* in 1912.

Big-City Wonders   51

Though there were closer ports, many of the dead were brought here to be buried. Some could be identified but most of the markers bare only a number.

Another Halifax oddity is the Chapel of Our Lady of Sorrows at South and Park streets, which was built in a single day by 2,000 men. Then there is the heather that grows in Point Pleasant Park, a tranquil preserve in the south end of the city. The heather was apparently introduced by sailors who made a practice of shaking the stuffings out of their mattresses on the Point in order to refill them with fresh grasses. The stuffings contained heather seeds, which have taken hold almost nowhere else in North America. Also stop at Historic Properties, the section of the waterfront between Duke and Buckingham streets which has been restored to look as it did in its heyday when privateers sailed from its wharves to attack French and American shipping and build vast fortunes. The restored warehouses, which at one time were to be torn down to make way for a freeway, now house some of the finest boutiques and restaurants in Halifax. Here you can also climb aboard the *Bluenose II*, a full-sized replica of the famous racing schooner pictured on the backs of our dimes, for a summer tour of the splendid harbor.

20. Water Street, St. John's

In St. John's, Newfoundland, when you wander along Water Street, the city's main drag, you are on the oldest shopping street in the New World. It runs through a beach where Portuguese fishermen used to barter goods a century before the Pilgrim Fathers set sail for America. Also on Water Street you will find a plaque identifying the spot where the British Empire began. It was there that Sir Humphrey Gilbert took possession of Newfoundland in the name of Queen Elizabeth I, thus establishing Britain's first overseas colony.

21. Plains of Abraham, Quebec

In Battlefield Park in Quebec city, you find yourself wandering over the same Plains of Abraham where Wolfe and Montcalm met in the most important battle in Canadian history. Tablets mark the course of the battle.

22. World's Most Active Underground City

Montrealers know they have the world's most active underground city, but visitors are usually surprised by its vastness. There are well over 3 miles of shops, restaurants, hotels and pubs in the maze of underground streets and plazas connected to the city's Metro (subway) system. They permit you to wander freely without ever once going out of doors, not a bad idea on winter days in Montreal that hit 20 below.

Everyone in the world knows that Toronto, a city of 3,000,000, sprouts the world's tallest free-standing structure, which, at 1,815 feet, towers over a downtown filled with the highest skyscrapers in the British Commonwealth. But there is a lot beneath that CN Tower that comes as a real surprise to visitors. For example, the 30 live theaters that make this city the most active city for stage performances on the continent, except for New York.

23. Kensington Market, Toronto

Then there's the Kensington Market, an old-world-style shopping area sprawling over 5 or 6 blocks around Augusta and Baldwin avenues. It started out as a Jewish market area of kosher butchers, fish stores and outdoor new and used clothing stalls. Now there are more Portuguese than Jewish merchants, besides Italian, Greek and Jamaican. Where else can you get quail eggs or 25 kinds of salami in one store or hear salesmen in 5 different languages talking up a sale within a single block?

24. The Island, Toronto

Visitors may know that the Science Centre in Toronto is one of the world's best and that the Oriental Collection at the Royal Ontario Museum is so good that the Japanese borrowed from it for Expo '70 in Osaka. But they can't understand why no one told them about The Island. People in Toronto take their island for granted, seldom realizing that it is a unique piece of downtown greenery just a few minutes by ferry from the skyscrapers of Canada's busiest city. The island is really 3 islands formed more than a century ago when waves cut them adrift from the rest of the city. Now those islands offer swimming beaches, a 612-acre playground, a barnyard filled with animals children can pet, bicycling trails, boating of all sorts—and not a car in sight. You just get yourself to the foot of Bay Street to hop a ferry to the island.

Some visitors don't realize Toronto has its own castle, a hilltop 98-room affair that eccentric millionaire Sir Henry Pellat had built in 1914 for $3 million. Casa Loma's stable was built of maple and mahogany and had secret passages for the servants so Sir Henry wouldn't have to meet them in the hall. You'll be glad to hear he went broke and the city took over his castle which you can visit daily year-round.

25. Canada's Wonderland

One thing that was always missing from the Canadian scene was a major Disneyland-style amusement park; but in May 1981 an immense, 108-million-dollar theme park opened just 20 miles northwest of Toronto's City Hall. Canada's Wonderland has been built around an artificial mountain surrounded by castles, pagodas, 35 rides and 40 places to eat in 5 theme areas. These sprawl across 320 acres on the east side of Highway 400 between Rutherford Road and Major MacKenzie Drive. The park is expected to attract between 2 and 3 million visitors in its first year of operation. Animated Hanna-Barbera cartoon characters such as Fred Flintstone and Yogi Bear mingle with the crowds in theme areas that whisk you from medieval England to frontier Canada. The park is open daily from mid May until Labor Day.

Big-City Wonders

When you reach the prairies, you think you've seen the last of big boats. But in Winnipeg, you can hop aboard a paddlewheeler for a cruise down the Red River to Lower Fort Garry, 19 miles north of town. Fort Garry is the only stone fort remaining from the days of the fur trade to have survived almost intact.

26. Golden Boy, Winnipeg

Part of seeing the offbeat side of Canada is discovering something about landmarks that even the natives of an area don't know. Such as the story behind Winnipeg's famed Golden Boy.

This gilded statue stands atop the dome of Manitoba's neo-classical Legislative Building and, before a gush of skyscrapers spurted in downtown Winnipeg, dominated the entire city. With a torch in one hand and a sheaf of wheat under the other, the Golden Boy is a heroic figure that has become the symbol of the whole province. But his history is even more heroic than most Winnipeggers, who look up at him daily, suspect.

He was cast in a foundry in France just before the start of World War I. When hostilities began, the place where he was made was demolished by German shelling. He was one of the few things in the factory to escape unscathed. He was quickly put on a ship bound for New York but alas, it was commandeered as a troop ship so he spent two years sailing back and forth through torpedo-infested waters before landing and heading west and making it to the top.

The surprise of Regina is that it turns out to be an oasis in a vast belt of wheat in more ways than one. Wascana Centre, a 2,000-acre parkland right in the heart of the city, houses a fine theater, the government buildings, a bird refuge, a lake where you can go sailing and the prairie homestead of John Diefenbaker, the first westerner to become prime minister of Canada.

In Calgary, if you have children in tow, take them out to the zoo not so much to see the live animals as to see the Dinosaur Park, filled with immense 32-foot-high reproductions of the great reptiles that roamed the prairies before the time of man.

In Edmonton, head down to the banks of the North Saskatchewan River, which the city straddles. This valley has been turned into a 17-mile-long parkland filled with picnic sites, golf courses and ponds and is also the home of 4 glass pyramids filled with plants from each of the world's different climatic zones.

Visitors to Vancouver should know that it has one of the great in-city parks anywhere in the world and North America's second largest Chinatown (after San Francisco's). Stanley Park has a backdrop of snow-capped mountains and is bordered by the sea on three sides. In summer it is alive with people cycling or walking 50 miles of trails, taking in a cricket match, mimicking the penguins at the zoo, whale-watching at the aquarium or gazing up at giant evergreens that were there before Columbus discovered America. Chinatown, centered along Pender Street, just east of the main business district, has some fine Chinese restaurants and also large and small emporiums of Oriental offerings, ranging from pressed duck to festive lanterns.

Take along an old sweater and a pair of sneakers when you head to that west coast metropolis so that you can do some inexpensive salmon fishing right out there in pacific waters. All you do is head out to Horseshoe Bay where the ferry boats depart for Vancouver Island. There you can hire a modern outboard and salmon fishing rod, have a quick lesson from the dock staff on baiting your hook and get instructions on the best places to try out there on Howe Sound. Then away you go on an adventure that won't set a couple of landlubbers back more than $25.

When you get back, you will be ready for the 2 big aerial thrills Vancouver has to offer—the swing and sway of the Capilano Suspension Bridge and the ride to the top of Grouse Mountain, a winter ski area that overlooks downtown Vancouver. Both can be reached easily by taking the Lions Gate Bridge to North Vancouver and turning north onto Capilano Road.

27. Capilano Suspension Bridge, Vancouver

The bridge is on your left as you drive up through one of the most desirable residential areas of Greater Vancouver. Before you lay eyes on the bridge you will hear the shrieks of people already crossing it—and you will soon see why. This 450-foot footbridge, one of the longest in the world, seems to sway in the breeze 230 feet above the spectacular Capilano River canyon. The bridge is perfectly safe and thousands work up enough nerve to cross it on sunny summer days. Still, there is no need to be ashamed if you are one of several dozen a day who refuse to set foot on it once you see it dance in the breeze.

28. Grouse Mountain, Vancouver

The Grouse Mountain aerial circus is just up the road and there is a large parking lot to handle the all-year traffic. For even when the ski season ends, the mountain offers one of the best big-city views in the whole country. The first part of the run, a cable car takes you to the 3,600-foot level; it departs every 10 minutes. From there, you can climb aboard a chairlift that takes you to the 4,000-foot level for a superb view of the city, sprawling out ¾ of a mile below you. This is a good spot to see hang-gliding demonstrations offered on fair days. On the 3,600-foot level, there are picnic tables and nature trails and a new mountainside rollercoaster ride.

29. Marine Museum, Victoria

No one with a nautical bent should leave Victoria without taking a look at the Marine Museum in downtown Bastion Square. It's one of the nicest you'll find anywhere, containing the legendary Indian war canoe *Tilikum* in which Captain J. C. Voss sailed from Victoria to Margate, England. The craft was rotting in the mud of the Thames, its incredible journey forgotten, when some of those old sea captains who now make Victoria their home rescued it.

Many visitors head to Victoria primarily to see Butchart Gardens, 12 miles north of town. It's English, Japanese, Italian and sunken gardens may well add up to Canada's best man-made beauty spot. But few people realize that right in downtown Victoria they can visit the smashing Beacon Hill Park, with its 150 acres of flowerbeds, for free.

CHAPTER VIII
Two Capital Ideas

Ottawa, the capital of Canada, has many popular tourist attractions. Visitors take a free guided tour of the stately Parliament buildings, ride to the top of the Peace Tower, watch the Changing of the Guard on the lawns of Parliament Hill, drive the flower-bedecked parkways on either side of the Rideau Canal, tour the National Arts Centre and the National Gallery and then pick from an assortment of downtown attractions: Laurier House, home of 2 prime ministers, the National Museums of Man and Natural Sciences, the National Postal Museum and the Mint. If they have children in tow, they also drive out to St. Laurent Boulevard to see the National Museum of Science and Technology, with its collection of steam engines, vintage automobiles and computer gadgetry. All are worthwhile and, best of all, most of them are free.

But 2 fine attractions are missed by many visitors to Ottawa, the first because they don't know about it, the second because it is all but hidden away. So when you go to see the capital don't miss the chance

Two Capital Ideas   61

to meet the most punctual man in Canada and to take in one of the world's best collections of vintage planes.

30. The Noonday Gun

The most punctual man in Canada is the chap who fires the noonday gun. He has to be because everyone in Ottawa from the prime minister on down sets his watch by it. The mail may not get through if it snows hard enough but you can count on the man who fires the noonday gun. It goes off exactly at noon 6 days a week and at 10 A.M. on Sundays as it has for more than a century. Its blast can be heard all around the city. Its firing is entrusted to handpicked members of the Canadian Corps of Commissionaires, the men who help guard the Houses of Parliament. You will find the 9-pound, muzzle-loading cannon at Major's Hill Park, just behind the Chateau Laurier Hotel. It is close to the spot where the city of Ottawa (originally known as Bytown) was founded. It was John A. Macdonald, Canada's first prime minister, who instituted the noonday gun firings there in 1869.

About half an hour before noon each day, the commissionaire shows up and loads the cannon with 1¼ pounds of gunpowder. As the Peace Tower Clock, certainly not accurate enough for him, reaches quarter to 12, he pulls out a radio receiver tuned to the National Research Council time signal and raises the antenna to bring in the beeps. As a voice announces a minute to go, he puts one hand on the lever of a battery-operated detonator and gets ready to fire. At the proper dash, he presses the button and ducks his head. The roar is a shocker, loud enough to send the few onlookers who show up a few steps back, some onto the seats of their pants. You'll notice that the bongs of the Peace Tower clock are often over a second or two before the noonday gun blasts off. But then, everyone in Ottawa knows that the noonday gun is the only really accurate timepiece in town.

31. The National Aeronautical Collection

The second Ottawa attraction many people miss is the National Aeronautical Collection. It is one of the world's best collections of vintage aircraft, including some originals from the early days of flight that are the only ones left of their kind. The collection is great. What isn't is the location of the planes. They are housed in a couple of old hangars at Rockcliffe Airport in a location that even Ottawa natives have trouble finding. To get there, you take the Queensway to St. Laurent Boulevard, then follow St. Laurent north almost to the Ottawa River where you will spot the hangars on your left at Beechwood Avenue. Admission, as in the case of nearly all Ottawa museums, is free.

Three hangars house the collection's 95 aircraft but one is for storage and workshops. The other two contain the display areas, with World War I and civilian aircraft from the '20s and '30s in one and World War II aircraft and a few more modern ones in the other. Some are original goods and others are replicas of planes no longer in existence. The World

Two Capital Ideas

War I planes include a twin-engine bomber that may be the only one to survive. There is a rare Sopwith Snipe, generally regarded as the best fighting plane to be developed in World War I. It was used in the film *Hell's Angels* before being acquired by the collection. Other notable vintage craft are a BE2C, of the type that was rushed into action to defend Britain against Zeppelin airships; an Avro 504K, which actually went on bombing raids; a Sopwith Triplane and a replica of the Nieuport flown by Victoria Cross-winning air ace Billy Bishop. The other hangar offers closeups of such well-known World War II planes as Hawker Hurricanes, Spitfires and Mustangs.

For many years, aircraft buffs have been attempting to have a first-rate museum built to contain the collection and other vintage aircraft such as the Silver Dart, the replica of the plane that made the first flight in Canada. It and other notable relics are now scattered among various Ottawa museums. Until that new museum comes, however, the National Aeronautical Collection will remain part of Offbeat Canada.

Don't expect your member of parliament to tell you about it—but Canada's best girl-watching is to be found almost in the shadow of the Peace Tower. Just head for the Sparks Street Mall any sunny summer and you'll find this pedestrians-only avenue packed with government stenographers having lunch among its beer gardens and boutiques. Street musicians supply the background music.

CONTACT

For city map and guide to all Ottawa attractions, write to Canada's Capital Visitors and Convention Bureau, 251 Laurier Ave. W., Suite 1009, Ottawa, Ontario K1P 5J6.

CHAPTER IX

Oddities Along the Trans-Canada

Many of Canada's most unusual attractions lie right along the Trans-Canada Highway, that 5,000-mile Main Street Canada that arches across the country like a rainbow stretching from sea to sea. Yet most of them are missed by the passing parade.

32. Ouimet Canyon

Most travelers heading across the top of Lake Superior on the Trans-Canada sail right past Ouimet Canyon without realizing it's there. Yet it is a canyon whose vital statistics are even more impressive than Dolly Parton's. It is 2 miles long, 500 feet across and 400 feet deep. In fact, it is large enough that the province of Ontario once had a plane fly through it to produce some dramatic film footage on her tourist attractions. Canada's miniature version of the Grand Canyon is just 42 miles east of Thunder Bay. You turn north off the Trans-Canada and take a secondary road for 8 miles to the edge of the canyon. When I first made the trip in 1973 that road was one of the worst in the whole country, fit only for a four-wheel-drive vehicle after any substantial rainfall. Now the province has realized the potential of Ouimet and is finally putting in a good road.

Once you reach the canyon, don't expect to find anything that wasn't there when the Ojibway Indians first laid eyes on the place, long before Columbus came to America. Except for a small parking lot, almost nothing has been added to disturb the canyon's primeval splendor. It is scary enough at the top that some people crawl to the edge to peek over. When they do, they notice that even in this remote corner of Canada, man has managed to make his mark in much the same way he did when he went to the moon and left his garbage behind. Several years ago someone stole a truck and pushed it over the edge. Its remains can still be seen on the rocks below.

Getting to the bottom of the canyon is no mean trick. There's a lake at one end with a rough trail running along its edge. But when I followed the trail I found that it ran smack into the canyon wall. One would have to take a canoe along the trail in order to get to the canyon floor, which because of its strange geology produces some Arctic plants found nowhere else south of the tundra. Even geologists aren't sure how Ouimet Canyon was born. Is it simply a gigantic fault in the earth's surface or did some mighty glacier carve it out?

Though there's nothing else quite as spectacular as Ouimet, much of the terrain that the Trans-Canada (Highway 17) cuts through north of Lake Superior is dramatic, with huge outcroppings of the

Precambrian Shield supplying fine vantage points over both the largest of the Great Lakes and some of the 30,000 inland lakes that lie just to the north.

33. Kakabeka Falls

Just off the Trans-Canada Highway near Thunder Bay is a mighty cataract that has been dubbed the "only on Sunday waterfall." Kakabeka Falls is 225 feet wide and 128 feet deep and is an awesome spectacle when it is at full throttle. Unfortunately for spectators, that's not too often. One of northern Ontario's major hydro-electric dams is located just above the falls; it cuts the flow of the Kaministiquia River almost in half, except on Sunday when water is allowed to pour over the full falls. Even at half-flow, however, Kakabeka is worth a stop. It pours into one of the most magnificent gorges you'll ever come across and hasn't even a shred of the honky-tonk atmosphere that sometimes turns Niagara Falls into a three-ringed circus.

34. Carberry Desert

If you follow the Trans-Canada through the Prairies, you will need a few stops to relieve the boredom of driving through an endless sea of wheat. Fortunately, there are some good offbeat stops you can make—such as the Carberry desert in Manitoba. Situated right in the middle of the province's breadbasket, the desert is just an 18-mile side trip south of the Trans-Canada along Highway 258 in the area of

Spruce Woods Provincial Park. This is a desert that has everything a Hollywood producer could ask for—rolling dunes, shifting sands, ridges of hard-packed sand waves and crumbling cliffs you literally have to crawl up on your belly. It's so much the way you dreamed deserts should be that you almost expect to see Lawrence of Arabia or at the very least Rommel and the Afrika Korps ride up over the next hill.

Strangely enough, this desert has remained a well-kept secret, even from Manitobans. That is because it is situated only a few miles from the Ministry of Defence's Shilo firing range and is technically part of the out-of-bounds area surrounding the range. But it has always been considered so safe that I once saw a soldier in a jeep showing two busloads of children over the dunes. To reach the desert, which covers a couple of square miles, take Highway 258 south from Carberry to the place where it is crossed by the Assiniboine River. You can park your car in a lot by the road and walk in through a bush of spruce and poplar.

35. The Cypress Hills

When the Trans-Canada rolls into Saskatchewan, many travelers make a stop at the excellent Royal Canadian Mounted Police Museum in Regina and then keep right on going. Just before they leave the province they bypass the tallest mountains east of the Rockies without even knowing they are there. The Cypress Hills rise 4,700 feet above the unforgivingly flat prairie through which you have been driving. They are now the centerpiece of one of Canada's best provincial parks; here you will find the great stands of lodgepole pine that the French fur traders who named the place mistook for cypress. The Cypress Hills are just 25 miles south of the Trans-Canada on Highway 21.

36. Dinosaur Provincial Park

When they reach Alberta, people are usually in such a rush to get to the Rockies that they miss one of the world's great links with our prehistoric past—Dinosaur Provincial Park. More than 100 major fossil finds have been made in this park, which is located in the eerie Red Deer River Badlands. These include the remains of 30 different species of dinosaur that for 65 million years roamed that area when it was at the edge of a semitropical inland sea. Since the first dinosaur bones were discovered here in 1884, fossils from the Alberta badlands have made their way into the collections of 30 major museums around the world. The park is looked on as such a treasure house of links with the prehistoric past that the United Nations had declared it a World Heritage Site, one of only four in Canada.

During the summer months there are guided bus tours and fossil safaris in the park. Nature trails wind through the badlands, dinosaur quarries and displays. The park is just 31 miles northeast of Brooks, which is right on the Trans-Canada.

While in the area you should also drive the 30-mile Dinosaur Trail beginning and ending near Drumheller, which lies some 400 feet below the surrounding prairie in the valley of the Red Deer River. Here you will find petrified wood in abundance, fossil shells, berries and cones preserved from prehistoric times and whole beds of ancient oysters. This is also the land of the giant hoodoos, weird mushroom-shaped rocks carved by eons of wind and water action. The best collection of them is at East Coulee, eight miles east of Drumheller.

37. Hell's Gate

When you reach British Columbia, heading west on the Trans-Canada, you think you have had your fill of mountain scenery. Then you come to Hell's Gate in the Fraser River canyon and all those mountains that have kept their proper distance suddenly close in on you so that you have to crane your neck to see the sky. Once Indians made their way through this canyon on pegs pounded into the cliffs but modern man has pushed 2 railways and the Trans-Canada through the same space. When you look down you see the violent Fraser River that cut this immense gulch out of solid rock. Stop and take an aerial car ride across the canyon to get an idea of the might of this river that drains a quarter of the area of British Columbia, pushing 34 million gallons a minute through on average. Then stop to take a look at the immense fish ladder built to assist 2 million salmon a year through Hell's Gate. This is one part of Offbeat Canada that is difficult to miss as it is located right on the Trans-Canada. Just take this as a warning not to pass through at night and miss one of the country's major scenic wonders in your rush to the sea.

38. Saint-Jean Port Joli

If you head east on the Trans-Canada from the hole in the ground called Ouimet where we started this chapter, you will also find plenty of offbeat attractions that won't take you more than a few miles off the highway. In Quebec, after you have followed the Trans-Canada through the joy of Montreal and the charm of Quebec city, there's an extremely worthwhile stop to be made on the south shore of the St. Lawrence River at the village where just about everyone whittles while he works. It's called Saint-Jean Port Joli and it lies just north of the Trans-Canada, 60 miles east of Quebec city.

This is the woodcarving capital of Canada, with some 250 residents making their living that way. The Bourgault family of three brothers started the whole thing, whittling away to amuse themselves and put in the hours as they worked at such jobs as lighthouse keeper. Finally, they had a room filled with their work. A government official who was amazed at its quality helped get them started at displaying and selling it. That was during the depression and some of the pieces that the brothers had spent hours on went for just $1. Now some have been resold for as much as $3,000. The woodcarving shops line both sides of the river road as it runs through town and you can see carvers at work any summer day you stop by. In fact, wouldn't you know it, some of them even carve on an assembly line with one person doing ears and another arms or legs.

39. The Kissing Bridge

When the Trans-Canada rolls into the Maritimes, it soon begins to follow the beautiful Saint John River, often perambulating along banks where cattle graze and willows lean lazily over the river as if to drink. At Hartland, it brings you to the world's longest kissing bridge. In horse-and-buggy days, kissing bridges were a dime a dozen in eastern Canada and the U.S. Now you are lucky to see one in a month of traveling. Except, that is, in New Brunswick where 88 of the original 400 covered bridges are still in use, including this 1,282-foot span which crosses the Saint John River at Hartland, right beside the Trans-Canada.

Kissing bridges got their name because they created a nice, dark recess for lovers as their buggies passed through or as they strolled across a river. In fact, however, their builders had no such thing in mind. The roof and sides were built to protect the timber supports of the bridge from the constant wetting and drying that would have rotted them. In winter snow had to be shoveled onto the planking so a horse could pull a sleigh across more easily. It was not the planking but the support beams that needed the protection.

40. Magnetic Hill

When the Trans-Canada passes Moncton, take the time to try out Magnetic Hill if you have children along. All you do is drive to the botton of the hill and put your car in neutral. Suddenly, it apparently rolls back up the hill as if drawn by some magnetic force. You know it's all an optical illusion but children think it's magic.

41. Alexander Graham Bell Museum

The Nova Scotia section of the Trans-Canada avoids the thing I would tell anyone to do in that province—follow the coast. That's where the real Maritimes lie, in the salt-sprayed fishing villages that cling to its rocky seashore. The plan I advise is to go first to Peggy's Cove, near Halifax, just about everyone's choice as Canada's most picturesque fishing village. Then follow the coast in search of one you like even better. That could turn out to be Neil's Harbour or Arichat in Cape Breton, Little Harbour, 50 miles east of Halifax, or Lunenburg from which the original *Bluenose,* pictured on the back of the Canadian dime, sailed out to defeat all comers in schooner races. But at least the Trans-Canada takes you to the Alexander Graham Bell Museum, by far the most interesting museum in the Maritimes, in my book. It is filled with some 1,000 items dreamed up by the inventive mind of the man who gave us the telephone. There are contraptions to desalinate water and probe for bullets and an old sewing machine that Bell used to transform Edison's plaything—the phonograph—into the beginning of a viable recording industry. There are experiments dealing with the first flight in Canada, which took place at Baddeck, and with the hydrofoils Bell worked on. There is no admission charge.

Baddeck, by the way, is the starting point for the 184-mile Cabot Trail, a cliffhanger of a road that circles the Cape Breton highlands, often clinging to cliffs that hang over an angry sea.

42. Woodleigh Replicas

An offshoot of the Trans-Canada takes you, via ferryboat, onto Prince Edward Island where the best thing you've got going for you is that you are never more than 30 minutes from a warm ocean beach—in summer, that is. But if you're looking for an offbeat attraction, try Woodleigh Replicas near Burlington, a half-hour's detour off the Trans-Canada. Here the Johnstone family has built replicas of almost every famous building in Britain—the Tower of London, Glamis Castle, Shakespeare's birthplace, York Minster Cathedral, and St. Paul's. Most are built from the original plans and some of them are large enough for you to go inside for a look around. The Tower even has a full-sized replica of the Crown Jewels. Admission is $3 for adults, $1.25 for children.

When you take the 80-mile sea journey by car ferry to Newfoundland, you will find the Trans-Canada sweeping grandly through the middle of nowhere. The idea is to get off it a few times whenever it nears the south or north coasts and follow a road down to one of the former outports. Pick any road you want. In Newfoundland, the outport you fall in love with is the one you find for yourself.

CONTACT

For information on the whole Trans-Canada Highway and its sidetrips, write to the Canadian Government Office of Tourism, Ottawa, Ontario K1A 0H6.

CHAPTER X

Happy Trails

43. Trail Rides in the Rockies

The 12 people waiting to mount their horses at the trailhead near Banff, Alberta were a mixed bag indeed. One young woman had her own string of jumping horses back in Ontario; two regularly went to a stable back home for weekend riding; six said they used to ride but had hardly been on a horse in fifteen years; and two couldn't remember mounting up since they had their pictures taken on a pony as children. Then there was the obviously fit, 62-year-old visitor from Germany who said that, as far as he could recall, he had never been on horseback in his life. Yet all of them were enthusiastically, if nervously, preparing to mount up for a week-long pack trip into the Canadian Rockies. What's more, their group was more typical than you would suspect of the thousands who take holidays on horseback. More than a dozen outfitters now offer pack trips into the Rockies and nearly all of them are willing to take completely inexperienced riders as long as they are in good physical condition.

Trail riding is one of the best ways to see Offbeat

Happy Trails

Canada. It takes you into regions that cars can't penetrate and mountain valleys that are out of reach of most hikers. Trips that head into the Rockies from Banff, Rocky Mount or Jasper take you to the base of 9,000-foot-high peaks, across mountain streams where cut-throat trout are waiting to be caught and beside waterfalls that tumble hundreds of feet. It's not unusual to spot bear cubs brawling their way across the trail in front of you or a lonesome elk staring silently down at you. You come on deep blue mountain lakes that haven't so much as a beer can thrown into them.

On the trail, you wake up to the smell of fresh-perked coffee and the sizzle of bacon and you have to watch out for mountain goats that would like to muzzle into your noontime wiener roast. Your nights may be spent in a mountain lodge, a log cabin or a tent, depending on how much you shell out for your pack trip. No matter which kind of trip you pick, you can count on spending a couple of nights around a campfire while someone strums a guitar or tells you about the West the way it used to be.

You can also count on being awfully sore after the first day's riding, although most outfits restrict the first day to 5 or 6 hours in the saddle. It's a good idea to prepare for a holiday on horseback by heading out to a riding stable for a couple of leg and posterior preparation sessions. Some wranglers suggest a few exercises you can do at home to get ready for a trip, such as kneeling on the rug with your feet crossed behind you and then raising and lowering your body. Do this exercise faithfully and you can still count on aches and pains aplenty after your first day. But the good news is that most people get over them after a day or two in the saddle and by the end of the third day even walk without a limp.

There are several kinds of pack trip you can take. The ultimate experience is one that has you following an extensive trail and setting up camp each night in a different place. However, this kind of trip—and custom trips where you hire a guide to take you where few others have ever been—are generally for more experienced riders. The usual type of pack trip for beginners, and even veteran riders seeking a mountain outdoors adventure, is what is known as the base camp trip. This is one in which the outfitter has set up a more or less permanent camp, though he may change the location from year to year. Riders follow the trail to the camp, with maybe an overnight stop en route, then use the camp as a base for rides into the mountains during their stay.

Guides, who invariably look like Gary Cooper, know their string of horses and their territory as well as you know your car and the throughway that gets you to work. They are adept at picking out a horse best suited to your riding experience and they will take you to the best fishing rivers, the best photographic viewing spots and the places where you are likely to see a moose stopping for a morning drink. Besides the riders under his care, the guide is in charge of a string of pack horses that bring in the food supplies, duffel bags of each rider and, in cases where tents must be set up, camping gear. You are expected to bring your own warm sleeping bag, a ground sheet and pad if you want one, 2 changes of

Happy Trails 79

clothing, raincoat and rain footwear and toiletry items. Generally, riders are limited to 30 pounds of duffel that should be packed into a tubular-shaped canvas or nylon bag. Don't forget to tag it well because on the trail duffel bags look as much alike as blue flight bags do on an airport carousel. Meals are always included in the price of your trip; they are hearty affairs—beans, big chunks of beef or stew, fried trout caught along the way, fresh-baked biscuits—all made by one of the guides who doubles as a cook. Riders aren't required to pitch in with the chores but you will get a lot more out of an experience like this if you help unsaddle the horses or set up the tents.

Expect to pay $55 to $70 a day for a trail ride in July and August. Some outfitters give reduced rates in June and September and discount rates for family groups.

CONTACT

More than a dozen first-rate outfits offer Rockies pack trips. One worth singling out is Trail Riders of the Canadian Rockies, a nonprofit organization that organized its first ride in 1923. Base camps of tall teepees are set up in the Cascade Valley one year and at the base of Mt. Assinaboine the next, with circle rides of 12 miles or so taken each day. Write for information to Secretary-treasurer, Trail Riders of the Canadian Rockies, Box 6742, Station D, Calgary, Alberta T2P 2E6.

Other well-known outfitters working out of the Banff area include Warner & McKenzie Holiday on

Horseback, Box 2280, Banff, Alberta T01 0C0.
Paul Peyto Timberline Tours, Box 14, Lake Louise, Alberta T0L 1E0.
For the Jasper area
Ron Moore's Skyline Trailrides, Box 208, Jasper, Alberta T03 1E0.
Wald Olson's Tonquin Valley Amethyst Lake Pack Trips, Box 508, Jasper, Alberta T0E 1E0.
Gordon Dixon's Jasper Wilderness and Tonquin Valley Pack Trips, Box 550, Jasper, Alberta T0E 1E0.
Three-day trips in Jasper are offered by
Ed Regnier, Miette Trailrides, Box 496, Edson, Alberta T0E 0P0.
For Rocky Mount (Rocky Mountain House)
Ed McKenzie's Trailswest, Box 971, Rocky Mountain House, Alberta T0M 1T0.
Sam Sands' Trail Rides, Rocky Mountain House, Alberta. T0M 1T0.
Diamond Jim Mountain Rides, Rocky Mountain House, Alberta, T0M 1T0.
Alpine Trail Rides, Box 209, Caroline, Alberta. T0M 0M0.

For a complete listing of Alberta pack trip operators, write to Travel Alberta, Box 2500, Edmonton, Alberta T5J 0H4 and ask for a free *Visitors Accommodation Guide*. It lists all major pack-trip outfits.

44. Ontario Trail Rides

Ontario also offers pack trips though none of them comes close to hitting the peaks of a Rocky Mountain trail ride. Almaguin Trails offers both 5-day and weekend wilderness rides that can be booked through a travel agent. The weekend trip, costing about $140, is a good way of seeing if you and a horse can get along.

On weekend trips, you are picked up at the Yorkdale subway station in Toronto and driven in a converted school bus to Almaguin's base lodge on Deer Lake, 12 miles west of South River (close to the northwest corner of Algonquin Park). You rest for the night and then mount up for a true wilderness ride, following old logging trails through dense bush, across streams, over beaver dams and through bogs. Take along plenty of insect repellent; you'll need it. It is a 17-mile ride to a wilderness camp already set up in the bush by Almaguin staff, and you will be ready to hit the sack as soon you have supper. Next day, you ride back to the lodge over a different trail or, if you aren't up to it, get a drive back to the lodge in the food delivery truck. Almaguin takes both veteran riders and beginners but has found that not all beginners are ready for the tough trail the operators at first set up. So first-time riders may now choose between it and an easier course that follows some bush roads.

CONTACT
Almaguin Trails Horseback Expeditions, Box 1109, King City, Ontario L0G 1K0, or Box 608, South River, Ontario P0A 1X0.

There are splendid hiking possibilities right across Canada. Provincial and national parks have marked trails and usually offer opportunities in summer to hike with a naturalist. We can't deal with all the possibilities so we have selected two first-rate trails: one through the heart of the most populated part of Canada and one through one of the country's loneliest but most dramatically beautiful stretches.

45. Hiking the Bruce Trail

First, let's head for the heart of southern Ontario, where the Bruce Trail spins a 430-mile rustic route between some of Canada's largest cities. It starts in the lush fruit-growing area of the Niagara Peninsula and follows a footpath along the Niagara Escarpment to the little resort town of Tobermory at the tip of the Bruce Peninsula. The escarpment is a 450-million-year-old ridge of limestone rock that runs right through the city of Hamilton, skirts the western suburbs of Toronto and then heads through meadows, woodlands and farm fields to the rugged terrain of the Bruce Peninsula.

One of the beauties of the Bruce Trail is that it

can be tackled by the veteran hiker wanting to be tested by a long hike or by the beginner looking for a place to make a start. That's because the trail crosses many highways and rural concession roads, enabling you to hike for a week or just a couple of hours before rejoining the modern world. A foursome, for example, can drive to a spot along the trail where two of them get out and start hiking north. Then the other two drive to another point on the trail, say seven miles to the north, park the car, and start hiking south. When they meet the other couple they hand over the car keys and are met when they arrive at the southern starting point by the other couple, who have retrieved the car at the end of their hike and driven it back. Which brings up a point about hiking: it's a good idea to go in the company of at least one other person or any major hike and it's an even better idea to inform someone not involved with the hike what your itinerary and expected return time are. In the case of some northern and western parks, you are required to inform the staff of hiking plans. I was glad I did this once on a hike in Jasper because the man in charge suggested we carry a tin can with small stones in it tied to our belts. That way you don't surprise any bears, sometimes a fatal thing to do. We saw a bear scampering through the bush just ahead of us and were sure he was alerted to our presence by our makeshift rattle.

CONTACT

To hike the Bruce Trail you should have its handbook which maps out the trail and pinpoints shelters and campgrounds along the way. It is available for

$6 from the Bruce Trail Association, Box 44, Station M, Toronto, Ontario M6S 4T2. Families can join the association and take part in its planned outings for $10.

46. The Pangnirtung Pass

The Pangnirtung Pass is as remote as the Bruce Trail is handy. It is located in Auyuittuq National Park, on the Arctic Circle, 1,500 miles northeast of Montreal. But there isn't a more glorious hiking area than this one, which takes you to the edge of a remnant of the last ice age, Penny Ice Cap, 2,200 square miles of solid ice. Glaciers flow down from it into the valleys below and one of them, the Coronation Glacier, is a river of ice 20 miles long and 2 miles wide. That is why the park, which used to be called Baffin Island National Park, changed its name to Auyuittuq, the Inuit word for "the place that does not melt." The pass itself follows the valley of the Weasel River past 7,000-foot-high peaks and sheer 3,600-foot cliffs and across the Arctic Circle through valleys that in July are alive with yellow Arctic poppies and purple saxifrage, two of 100 forms of plantlife that survive in this valley. Along the trail (63 miles roundtrip), you won't spot much wildlife, because there isn't much there to support it. You might see lemmings, snowy owls, Arctic hare and the occasional polar bear. The trail runs along both sides of the Weasel River and takes you from Overlord, the park headquarters where overnight hikers must register, to Glacier Lake. It is a rugged trail where thigh-deep streams must be forded at times and

Happy Trails

where hikers are advised to rope themselves together to cross wide rivers and crevasses left by the ice. Even in July, the warmest month, temperatures will reach an average of only 44 degrees. No place for an amateur but a real challenge for the expert hiker looking for new worlds to conquer.

Getting there is also a challenge. You fly with Nordair from Montreal or Toronto to Frobisher Bay then take First Air to Pangnirtung. From the Inuit settlement there you either hike or take an Inuit freighter canoe or snowmobile 18 miles to the start of the trail.

CONTACT
Superintendent, Auyuittuq National Park, Pangnirtung, Northwest Territories X0A 0R0.

There's some Huckleberry Finn in all of us. The idea of floating away from the cares of the world is very appealing in this age of concrete jungles and expressway traffic jams. Fortunately, Canada is blessed with several million lakes and rivers and with seacoasts on three oceans and offers several kinds of holidays afloat that Huck would have given his best fishin' rod to have joined.

47. White Water Rafting

You are on the Chilko River of British Columbia and hanging on for dear life. That's because the big rubber and steel raft you and seven other landlubbers are riding has hit rapids so fierce the raft is almost standing on end. Ten-foot waves surge over you and you clutch even harder to the raft's hand ropes, thanking the Almighty that every passenger has to wear a lifejacket while running the rivers.

Then, as suddenly as you hit the rapids, you are out of them again, floating gently along, watching eagles circling above, listening as your boatman describes strange rock formations that only rafters or skilled canoeists get to see in the midst of British Columbia's roadless wilderness. Later, your raft passes through a canyon of the Fraser River where sheer cliffs rise 2,000 feet on either side. In all you spend 10 days on the river, camping each night along the banks, waking up to the sizzle of bacon, washing down dinner with a French liqueur and helping to clean up when you break camp so there is almost no sign that you were there. During those 10 days, you don't once think about the office, especially not when the raft is riding a rapid at a 45-degree angle.

There has been such an explosion of interest in river rafting since early accounts of trips through the Grand Canyon on the Colorado River first fired the public imagination that they are now offered in many parts of the U.S. and Canada. British Columbia is prime territory because it has so many rivers flowing down from the mountains into the sea with gorgeous canyons and more rapids than you can shake a paddle at. Moreover, sometimes twelve times as much water flows through canyons on the Fraser River as the Colorado carries through the Grand Canyon. So you see why British Columbians say they have the best rafting in the world.

Happy Trails

Rafting can be expensive since some trips include picking you up in Vancouver and flying you in by float plane to the place where you climb aboard the raft. Expect to pay close to $900 for a 12-day adventure of this sort. However, there are also one-day trips on the Fraser at Hell's Gate for as little as $45. Many five- and seven-day trips are offered. Anyone in good health can usually handle a rafting trip, though you must expect to be wet and uncomfortable at times. Some outfits will only take children 10 or over. Spills don't happen on many trips but you have to be prepared for them; your luggage, preferably duffel bags, is stored in waterproof containers.

CONTACT

John Mikes, who pioneered river rafting in British Columbia, runs Canadian River Expeditions, 845 Hornby St., Vancouver, British Columbia V6Z 1V1. Other active outfits include
Thompson Guiding Ltd., Riske Creek, British Columbia, VOL 1T0, Kumsheen Raft Adventures, Main St., Lytton, British Columbia, VOK 1Z0; McCook and Furniss Outfitters, Fort Ware, British Columbia V0J 3B0; Western Tours, Elgin Rd., White Rock, British Columbia V4A 2Y8 and Whitewater Adventures, 105 West 6th Ave., Vancouver, British Columbia V5Y 1K3. You can get a complete listing of rafting companies from Tourism British Columbia, 1117 Wharf St., Victoria, British Columbia V8W 2Z2. Also contact Tourism Yukon, Box 2703, Whitehorse, Yukon Y1A 2C6 for a list of outfitters offering rafting trips there.

48. Houseboat Holiday

You take many of the comforts of home along with you on a houseboat holiday—stove, refrigerator, flush toilet, maybe even a shower. It's like being in a recreational vehicle that floats instead of rolling along the highway, except that the construction of most houseboats also provides for a big sun deck.

You will find houseboats for rent in several parts of Canada but nowhere in the abundance that you find along Ontario's Trent-Severn Waterway system where one operator alone has 30 houseboats on the go. They can be rented even by people with no previous experience at handling a large power boat, which is one of the reasons lockmasters along the Trent system refer to these awkward craft as "Harvey Wallbangers." One marina operator located across the lake from a houseboat rental agency claims renters usually follow much the same pattern: "They take a trial run, gain their confidence and then zoom right across the lake into my dock."

But for the careful boatsman, houseboating can be the holiday of a lifetime—a week of moving from fishing hole to fishing hole, trolling all the way. A week when you wear your bathing suit most of the time and either cook your own meals or pull up to a dock to dine in town. You can anchor off an island and swim ashore or just lie on the rooftop sun deck in the happy knowledge that the phone can't ring and that any salesman who wants to drop by will have to row.

What sets the Trent-Severn area aside as one of

the world's best for houseboating is that it is a system of lakes, streams and canals linked by 45 locks. This system allows you to move easily from one lake to another and adds a real sightseeing dimension to your holiday. The Trent system stretches 232 miles from Lake Ontario to Georgian Bay and actually uses a waterway that the Indians canoed and portaged along as far back in history as the time of Christ. On the shores of Rice Lake you can pull your houseboat up to a dock in Serpent Mounds Provincial Park and visit one of Ontario's most offbeat attractions. The mounds are the mass graves of the Point Peninsula people, ancestors of the Iroquois, who came to the edge of the lake 2,000 years ago to harvest the wild rice and dine on its succulent clams. The graves, which are shaped like a gigantic snake wriggling its way down to the water, yielded a treasure trove of arrowheads and other tools used by these ancient Canadians. One of the unearthed graves has been left open, under a glass covering, showing the skull, bones, arrowheads and beads the way archeologists found them.

A short distance away you can put your houseboat into Peterborough's famed hydrolic liftlock where it floats like a toy duck in a bathtub while the whole lock is lifted 65 feet up to deposit you at the next level of the Trent system. The lift lock was regarded as one of the wonders of North America when it opened in 1904 and it still attracts tens of thousands of sightseers each year. It also draws many of the 170 houseboats now available for rest in Ontario.

CONTACT

Ontario Travel, Queen's Park, Toronto, Ontario M7A 2E5 publishes an annual booklet called *Boat Rentals in Ontario* which lists all the houseboats, as well as sailboats and large powerboats, available for rent. Expect to pay $200 to $500 a week, depending on the size of boat you choose and the time of year you rent. A big discount is given for early spring and late fall and at these times you may be able to rent by the weekend instead of by the week. Ontario Travel will also supply maps of the Trent-Severn system.

49. The Ferry Cruise

With two island provinces on her east coast and with her west-coast capital city located on an island, Canada depends heavily on ferry boats to glue her together. In the east the ferries of CN Marine take you to Prince Edward Island from New Brunswick and to Newfoundland on an 80-mile sea journey from North Sydney, Nova Scotia. In British Columbia, people and their cars are hauled to Vancouver Island, various Gulf Islands and up along the fjord-dotted northern B.C. coast by the 25 modern ferries operated by British Columbia Ferries as an extension of the provincial highway system.

Many of these boats take you to unusual parts of Canada but the one we are singling out is the 16-year-old *Queen of Prince Rupert*, the flagship of the British Columbia Ferries fleet. It offers you a gorgeous ocean cruise through spectacular fjord country for a fraction of what the many sleek cruise ships making the run to Alaska charge. It allows a vacationing motorist to do a combination mountain-and-sea journey as he circles B.C. In the off-season, from October to May, it offers bargain-priced return cruises to the nondriver.

In summer the *Queen* makes 20-hour runs up the Inside Passage from Port Hardy on Vancouver Island to Prince Rupert on the mainland, leaving from each port on alternate days. In the off-season it switches its operation to Vancouver, making 30-hour runs up to Prince Rupert and offering a 3-night return trip, including meals, stateroom, and a tour of Prince Rupert. These off-season cruises, especially in May and October when the weather is generally good, are an exceptional bargain at about $170 for each of 2 sharing a room. On the summer run from Port Hardy to Prince Rupert, 2 people and their car travel for about $150. By linking up with the *Queen*, using ferries between Vancouver and Nanaimo, you can avoid returning over the same route on a round trip to British Columbia. You take the Trans-Canada route west via Calgary to Vancouver, travel by ferries to Prince Rupert and then return east by the more northerly Yellowhead route that includes Jasper and Edmonton. The Inside Passage, by the way, is one of the world's great cruising grounds. At times the ferry appears to be surrounded on all sides by snow-capped peaks rising from the mainland and from the offshore islands.

CONTACT
British Columbia Ferries, Information and Reservation Centre, 1045 Howe St., Vancouver, British Columbia V6Z 2A9.

50. Cruise Ships

Once the Great Lakes and the St. Lawrence River were afloat with cruise ships but of late there has been only one liner offering summer sailings, the Soviet cruise ship *Alexandr Pushkin*. It sails out of Montreal on 7- and 9-day cruises that take you into the fjord lake Saguenay, to the birds and cliffs of Gaspé, to Prince Edward Island and Newfoundland and to the French Islands of St. Pierre and Miquelon. Rates range from about $400 to $800 for a one-week cruise on this ship where the maid who makes up your cabin may double as the concert pianist in the lounge in the evening.

CONTACT
March Shipping, 360 St. Jacques St., Suite 1400, Montreal Quebec H24 1P5.

You will find much more active cruising on the west coast where a dozen liners sail the Inside Passage between mainland British Columbia and its offshore islands on runs to Alaska. Many make a stop at Vancouver to pick up passengers and some ships depart from there. Travel agents can supply you with a list of ships making the run this summer.

Most other adventures afloat require that you be able to paddle a canoe, sail a boat or handle a cruiser. Rentals for all these are available in many parts of the country. Provincial tourist bureaus can usually supply a list of rental agencies.

51. Soaring Like an Eagle

To fly through the air like the birds is one of man's impossible dreams. But now it is actually something you can do without experience and without taking to a motorized aircraft. They call it gliding or soaring.

Gliding clubs are located in many parts of Canada but one of the most active areas is in rural southern Ontario where the rolling hills, sunny summer weather and unstable wind currents create the perfect atmosphere. Clubs are fine if you are a member. But what can someone who doesn't own a glider do to let more than his spirits soar? Simply head for your nearest gliding club and tell them you would like to go up as a passenger. Most gliders take two people and will welcome you aboard as a paying passenger. The normal charge is $20 for a trip that will last about 30 minutes.

Gliders get into the air by being pulled along by a tow plane. When the glider reaches the proper height, usually about 2,000 feet, and finds the right kind of upward air thrust, the glider pilot detaches the tow line and the two of you are on your own. He is trained to recognize where the upward columns of air, called "thermals," are. Small clouds, for example, are usually located at the top of a thermal. Also he can spot hawks riding a nearby thermal. If you catch a good one, it could take you as high as 8,000 feet (nothing, by the way, compared with the 40,000 feet that soarers reach in the Rockies of Colorado). When the fun is done, the pilot is able to guide his craft gently back to the field for a landing. Gliders are not like jet planes, which would fall from the skies like a stone if all their engines failed.

CONTACT
Ask your provincial tourist office for a lead to gliding clubs in your area. Unfortunately, few of them have telephones or office help as they are mostly social clubs. One we know of that takes passengers up is the Caledon Gliding Club, located about 45 miles northwest of Toronto, just north of Highway 24 on the 6th line of Caledon township west. It is a May-to-October adventure with most clubs active only on weekends.

CHAPTER XI
Offbeat Accommodation

You'll find the same look-alike chains of hotels and motels across Canada as you do in the United States. But you'll also find some rather unusual accommodation available to the traveler, including plush big-city apartments, country bed-and-breakfast establishments, family-run hotels in Quebec city where you can live a Left Bank existence and digs in Newfoundland outports where you can be a Newfie for a day.

52. All the Comforts of Home

You are in Vancouver and have just put in a full day of sightseeing. Now you've got your feet up, a 50-cent scotch on the rocks in your hand and are nibbling on a sandwich you just whomped up for yourself. You are wondering if you should go out on the town again tonight or make your own meal. That freedom of choice is one reason apartment vacations are catching on in Canada.

They are something to keep in mind the next

time you head for a major Canadian city. Apartments can now be booked by the day or the week as simply as hotels can. All you have to do is call your travel agent.

For, although many travelers aren't aware of it, an enterprising tour wholesaler named Tom Vincent has set up a network of short-term, fully furnished apartments for travelers to use in Vancouver, Calgary, Winnipeg, Toronto, Ottawa, Montreal and Halifax. Besides the fact that they are usually priced well below comparable hotel rooms, they allow you to have all the comforts of home on the road. Want a drink? Get ice and mix from the fridge and make your own—at about a quarter what you would pay for a room service or bar drink in a hotel. Make morning coffee while still in your pajamas. Eat a home-cooked breakfast and use the savings to splurge on dinners out on the town.

All apartments included in this network are within a short walk of public transportation and most of them are located right downtown. When you rent one by the week, your transfers to and from the airport are included in the rate. Some apartments in the plan insist that you book for a minimum of 3 days or a week, but daily bookings are accepted by others. There are bachelor apartments suitable for a single traveler or budgeting couple and 2-bedroom ones capable of housing a family. Maid service is usually included in the rate, although sometimes the service will be once a week, or 3 times a week, rather than daily. As in the case of hotels and motels, rates for these apartments go up in price each year. But they will cost you quite a bit less than comparable hotel space. For example, a couple can get a modest Montreal or Toronto apartment for as little as $30 a day and a fairly plush one in Vancouver, Calgary or Winnipeg for $45.

CONTACT
You can get detailed information from Tom Vincent's World Wide Villa Vacations, 175 Bloor St. E., Toronto, Ontario M4W 1C8. Or you can simply book one through a travel agent.

53. Canada's Left Bank

For my money, Quebec city is the top tourist city in Canada. Dramatically set in a split-level location above the St. Lawrence River, it is Canada's only walled city and one whose gray stones ooze both charm and history. Though skyscraper hotels now stand outside the walls of the old city like peeping toms at a nudist camp, the real show is inside those walls where a chateau of a hotel looks down on a chimney-potted skyline. It's a city of narrow streets where shopkeepers still come out to sweep their sidewalks and where beret-clad artists head home with their latest masterpiece rolled up under one arm and a loaf of french bread under the other. There's a whole street, Rue du Tresor, where artists hang their wares, and sidewalk cafés are sprinkled round and about in the most inconceivable places. You can sit down to eat in a 300-year-old stone cottage and find yourself on the very spot where Samuel de Champlain founded the city in 1608. Quebec city looks like the Left Bank of Paris, it smells like the Left Bank, tastes likes the Left Bank and, best of all, it allows you to live a Left Bank existence if only for a few days.

That's because this ancient city, where Wolfe met Montcalm in the most significant battle of Canadian history, is one of the few in Canada that offers a wide selection of modestly priced, family-run hotels and tourist homes. There are dozens of them within the walled section of the city, some even offering the garretlike rooms we identify with the Lost Generation in Paris. Most offer only the most basic accommodation but some even throw in a bit of charm—and the price is right.

The first time I booked into the Manoir La Salle on St. Ursule St., for example, I paid $5.40 for a single room. That was seven years ago. Today, minimum rates for a single have skyrocketed to $12 and Madame Therese Lachance, who owns the place, gets as much as $30 from a couple for her large downstairs room with a king-sized oak bed and its own bathroom. As in Paris, most Quebec Left Bank accommodation supplies only a wash basin in the rooms. Bath and toilet facilities are down the hall.

Mind you, there is a bit of Russian roulette to Quebec tourist-home accommodation. The room next door could be occupied by a Trappist monk or by a barber-shop quartet. I once stayed next door to a group of Quebec youngsters celebrating the fact that they had come of drinking age. Learned some new songs but didn't get much sleep.

One unfortunate aspect of these Quebec budget operations is that they don't serve up coffee and rolls as their Parisian cousins do. But old Quebec is such a compact place, dotted with all sorts of restaurants and cafés, that morning coffee is never more than a short walk away. (Which brings up a major travel tip. The new lightweight immersion heaters specially made for travelers are a great idea. They take up very little space in your luggage and allow you to boil a bit of water quickly to make instant coffee or a bowl of instant soup when no restaurant facilities are available.)

CONTACT
The small hotels and tourist homes in Quebec city are listed in a free guide called *Quebec Lodging* available from Ministère du Loisir, de la Chasse et de la Pêche, Direction des Communications, Case postale 22000, Quebec G1K 7X2. Once you arrive in Quebec, head to the city tourist office at 60 Rue d'Auteuil, just inside the St. Louis Gates, to pick up a free restaurant guide and a publication called *A Walking Tour of Old Quebec*. It will guide you easily to all the major sites.

54. The Country Circuit

If you want to shun big-city life as you make your way across Canada, you may be interested in the country bed and breakfast circuit that has now been firmly established from Newfoundland to British Columbia. It was achieved mostly through the efforts of John Thompson, a Quebec writer who wrote letters to hundreds of farm families across the country to prepare a guidebook called *Country Bed and Breakfast Places in Canada*. (Published by Deneau and Greenberg, it sells for $7.95.)

You can expect to pay about $15 single or $25 double to stay at a farm or ranch home. The prices include a full farm breakfast of bacon, eggs, and toast and coffee that keep on coming until you are filled. Some farm families are also willing to prepare supper for guests who are staying for more than a day. This is not, by the way, the same thing as the farm vacations described earlier. Some of the farm families on the country bed-and-breakfast circuit are too busy with chores or too limited in their accommodation to handle visitors seeking a complete holiday. They are more interested in overnight guests or people seeking a base for a couple of days of exploration in their area.

55. Newfie for a Day

St. John's may be the heart of Newfoundland but the province's soul lies in the hundreds of outports hidden away along its 6,000 miles of rock-ribbed coast. Once there were 1,300 of these tiny fishing hamlets where hardy fishermen and their families eked out a precarious existence. Most outports had no road to the outside world; the sea was their only highway. Outport families grew up in an isolation that was at the same time awful and splendid and gave the Newfoundlander his distinctive character. In modern Newfoundland, many of these outports have been abandoned while others have been linked by road to the Trans-Canada Highway, which sweeps

Offbeat Accommodation

565 miles across the island province. These roads allow the casual visitor to invade an outport and become a Newfie for a day. I once did that in the Eastport Peninsula village of Salvage and still consider it one of the most memorable days of my life.

I dined on cod tongues, seal soup, boiled moose and four kinds of vegetables, all washed down with a swig of homemade rhubarb wine. I went out jigging for cod with a fisherman who I saw working on his boat as I wandered along the village's only road. The meal cost under $3 and the fishing expedition just $5. The small museum in town was locked when I got there but children playing nearby ran and got the "curator" to open it up for me. Salvage (it rhymes with "rage") is typical of a Newfoundland outport, though more beautiful than most. It is built around an almost circular bay with neat little houses of every hue perched on rocks overlooking the bay. Most houses have fenced-in yards, not to keep the dog in but to keep the sheep that wander freely about the village out of the gardens. A rollercoaster of a road circles in front of the houses; on the other side, at the edge of the water, are the weatherbeaten fishing shacks, drying flakes and overturned dories that are Newfoundland's trademark. There is no motel and no restaurant, but in Canada's friendliest province, finding a place to sleep and a place to eat is just a matter of asking. Newfoundlanders are used to putting up strangers for the night and people in the village always seem to know who has a bed to spare. Not fancy, mind you, but usually scrubbed and tidy.

You can get a line on what the Newfies call "hospitality homes" by writing to the tourist department and asking for a free copy of *Where to Stay in Newfoundland*. It's a must guide for an island that has fewer hotels rooms than there are in the Royal York Hotel in Toronto.

CONTACT
Newfoundland Department of Tourism, Box 2016, St. John's, Newfoundland A1C 5R8.

56. On Campus

When their students are off for the summer, many Canadian universities and colleges rent rooms in their residences and dormitories. Rates can be as low as $8 single even in the heart of bustling Montreal. In many cases, the accommodation is spartan but some colleges offer meals and laundry facilities suitable for a family traveling on a tight budget.

CONTACT
For $1, you can get a directory of 40 universities offering accommodation in summer by writing to Anne Paulovich, Central College, Box 631, Station A, Scarborough, Ontario M1K 5E9.

57. In Jail

As in Europe, hostels offer the most economic accommodation for shoestring travelers. But you could end up in jail.

In Ottawa, the old Nicholas Street jail has been

converted into one of Canada's best hostels, one that is close to the museums, galleries and government buildings you came to see. In Banff, hostelers might find themselves spending the night in a large field tent that doubles as a hostel. It doesn't quite match the hostels in Europe where some are located in castles but the price is right, from $1.50 to $8 a night.

Hostels, by the way, aren't open only to the young. There is no age restriction in most of them and several even have family-room accommodation as well as the usual bunk or dormitory beds. Some hostels are open year-round; others only for the summer months. Some have laundromats and modern kitchen facilities while rustic ones offer wood stoves and outdoor plumbing.

CONTACT
Canadian Hostelling Association, 333 River Rd., Vanier City, Ottawa, Ontario K1L 8B9.

58. Inexpensive Digs in the Rockies

If you've ever arrived in Banff or Jasper in the summer, you'll know that "No Vacancy" signs are one of the most common sights. For these two towns, set amid the Rockies in Canada's most popular national parks, are among the country's most popular destinations. Hotels and motels are booked months ahead and even campgrounds become so crowded that Alberta radio stations warn motorists heading that way to book in elsewhere for the night.

But don't give up hope of staying in this rarified atmosphere on a summer visit. One of the best-kept secrets in both Banff and Jasper is the fact that there are a score of private homes that rent rooms and apartments by the day or week. A friend of mine booked into private homes in both Banff and Jasper, without prior reservations, last summer and is still raving about the deal he got. In Jasper, for example, he paid $20 a night for an apartment suite with its own private entrance, stove, refrigerator, bathroom, double bed, the works. And the landlady insisted on putting fresh flowers in his room every day.

Some of the private-home accommodation is available all year and some only during the summer tourist season. All are licensed to accept guests.

CONTACT
You can get a list of accommodations in private homes in Jasper by writing to the Jasper Park Chamber of Commerce, Box 98, Jasper, Alberta T0E 1E0.

For Banff, contact Banff reservations; Box 1628, Banff, Alberta T0L 0C0.

Discounts: Students get many discounts for accommodation. But few people know that young nonstudents under the age of 26 are also eligible for similar price breaks. All you need is a Youth International Educational Exchange Card, available for $5 from the Canadian Hostelling Association, 333 River Rd., Vanier City, Ottawa, Ontario K1L 8B9. CN hotels, such as the Chateau Laurier in Ottawa and the Nova Scotian in Halifax, offer a 50-percent reduction to card holders when there are rooms available. No advance reservations can be made at this discount rate but it can still be a big money-saver, especially on weekends when many big-city hotels have beds available because their business clients have gone home.

CHAPTER XII
Offbeat Dining

Montreal has nearly 5,000 restaurants and Toronto more than 4,000. When it comes to dining out in style, you can't beat these two cities. Why, in Toronto, you can go on an around-the-world gourmet trip even on a short stay, picking from a half dozen good Hungarian restaurants one night, hitting an Indian curry house or a Japanese steak house the next, dropping by a Russian restaurant on the third day and a Spanish on the fourth, then finishing the week among the scores of good French, Italian and Greek restaurants scattered around the city.

59. Lobster Suppers

But when it comes to seafood, even Toronto and Montreal take a back seat to the Maritimes in general and to tiny Prince Edward Island in particular. On this island, that the rest of Canada identifies more with potatoes than with seafood, you can sit down to a lobster dinner for as little as $10, including all the salads, fresh vegetables, apple pie and coffee you can down. For this is the home of the community lobster supper, offered nightly in community halls, church basements and the like.

In the little town of New Glasgow, P.E.I., lobster suppers have been served up in the recreational center for the past fourteen summers, with as many as 1,200 people showing up on a busy evening. New London serves lobster 7 nights a week in summer and Brackley Beach has been doing the same for ten years. New London also puts up a noontime smorgasbord that features chowder, scallops, salmon, tuna, cod and, of course, lobster. You can order wine with your lobster in St. Ann's where the nightly suppers are held in the parish hall. There you eat to the tune of organ music. At all halls serving lobster, you pay for extra portions of the featured attraction but usually are given second helpings of everything else free.

Some visitors to the island, and to other Maritime provinces, get their seafood feasts even cheaper. They pack one of those small camper shovels and a large pot in the trunk of their car, dig up their own clams, gather wood for a beachside fire and cook up a feast fit for a king. Some put the clams on a bed of moist sea grasses and let them steam in their own juices. There was a time when you could buy lobster from a fisherman at dockside in any Maritime fishing village and boil it in a pot of seawater. That's much more difficult these days because fishermen are no longer interested in making a quick sale to a tourist. But there are lobster pounds sprinkled around the coast of every down-east province where lobsters are kept alive in holding tanks. You can buy one to boil or sometimes get the operator of the pond to boil a couple up for you. I did that near Peggy's Cove last summer and paid $4 a pound for it.

60. Muck-a-Muck

Meanwhile, in west coast Vancouver, where the restaurant scene has brightened considerably in the past decade, there is one really unusual restaurant that's worth a try. It's called Muck-a-Muck and serves only the traditional fare of the British Columbia coastal Indians, featuring such items as fern shoots, salmon on twigs of cedar, cranberry juice and honey, rabbit and wild duck, and bannock, the whole-wheat Indian bread. Muck-a-muck is at 1724 Davie Street. Get there early in the evening, as reservations aren't taken.

61. A Taste of History

Aux Anciens Canadiens at 34 Rue St. Louis in the walled section of Quebec city is just one of three dozen fine restaurants in that city. But it is a special place for any visitor because it is located in the Jacquet House which dates from 1665 when the city was part of New France. It is a tiny cottage but one that manages to serve you 300-year-old history and fine food at the same time.

Aux Anciens Canadiens specializes in unsophisticated French home cooking, served amid antique furniture and sideboards by waitresses in aproned frocks and dustcaps. A complete dinner, including thick pea soup, crusty bread, a main course, dessert and coffee, will cost under $15. Make reservations; this is one of the most popular eateries in the whole city.

62. Top of the World

You can't see forever when you sit down to dine in the Top of Toronto, but you come closer to it here than anywhere because this revolving restaurant is more than 1,150 feet in the sky, about two-thirds of the way up the highest free-standing structure in the world—the CN Tower. On a clear day, you can see for 75 miles, taking in, among other things, the spray rising from Niagara Falls. Even when the weather is hazy you find yourself looking down on the rooftops of the tallest skyscrapers in the British Commonwealth and on planes landing below you at Toronto Island Airport.

The food in the restaurant is reasonably good but many critics have argued that it isn't up to the price—or the view. Expect to pay $50 a couple with wine for dinner and perhaps $35 for lunch. After dinner, you can shed some of those newly acquired pounds in an adjacent disco called Sparkles.

The tower itself is 1,815 feet, 5 inches high and looks not unlike a rocket ready to blast off from Cape Kennedy. It is so high that one man was able to parachute successfully from its top. Although built primarily as a communications tower by Canadian National, the government-owned railway, this space needle has two observation decks besides the restaurant and disco.

CHAPTER XIII

Our Glorious Past

63. The Viking Settlement

On Newfoundland's Great Northern Peninsula you can see absolute proof with your own eyes that the Vikings beat Columbus to America by about five hundred years. At L'Anse-aux-Meadows eight Norse buildings, dating from about the year 1000 A.D., have been unearthed by archeologists. They are thought to be the remains of the Vinland settlement founded by Leif the Lucky though, of course, there is no way of proving that Leif ever slept there.

Even before the ruins of the Viking settlement were finally discovered in 1961, historians had long believed that the Norsemen had stumbled on the New World centuries before Columbus set sail. The main evidence was contained in the Icelandic Sagas, those remarkable chronicles that even contain an eye-witness account of the Battle of Hastings. They tell of how Eric the Red discovered a frozen wasteland which he called Greenland in the hope of attracting colonists. And of how his son Leif Ericsson, known as the Lucky, sailed even farther to the west and discovered three new coastlines which he called Helluland (probably Baffin Island), Markland (probably Labrador) and Vinland (more than probably the extreme northern tip of Newfoundland). The Sagas say he built some large buildings there before returning to Greenland a year later.

One of the buildings unearthed at L'Anse-aux-Meadows is nearly 80 feet long and has 6 rooms. Searchers even found what they believe is a sauna bath because of the large number of cracked stones in the fireplace. Also uncovered was North America's first blacksmith shop. It was the materials found in the fireplace of this primitive smithy that enabled scientists, using radiocarbon tests, to establish the approximate age of the ruins.

Another major find was a tiny wheel, which Norse scholars were able to identify as a spindle whorl from a wool-spinning wheel. It established the fact that women had taken part in the L'Anse-aux-Meadows settlement. In fact the Sagas tell us that one of them gave birth to a boy, the first European born in America. The archeological digging, by the way, was done under the direction of Helge and Anne Ingstad, a Norwegian team. Though thrilled with the find, they avoided identifying it as Leif's Vinland without further proof.

The name Vinland has always puzzled historians because grapes don't grow as far north as Newfoundland. Some have argued that "vin" in Norse referred to grass as well as to grape vines. Perhaps the wild berries growing on the peninsula that even today's

Newfoundlander manages to turn into wine were identified as grapes by the Norsemen.

The Viking settlement is now a National Historic Park with an interpretation center where the life style of the settlers is depicted and reproductions of articles such as the whorl, a stone lamp and a bronze pin are displayed. The park is open from June 1 to Labor day. Located closer to a big city, L'Anse-aux-Meadows would attract millions of tourists. But sitting as it does on a distant peninsula, 270 miles over unpaved road from the Trans-Canada Highway, it attracts only a handful of visitors in search of an offbeat experience. If you are one of them, you will find camping at nearby Pistolet Bay Provincial Park and 2 motels and 2 tourist homes at St. Anthony.

If you are lucky, you may even spot an iceberg out on one of the bays. If you do, ask a fisherman to take you out for a close look. He usually will do so gladly for a small fee.

64. Archaic Indians Burial Ground

Highway 430, the coastal road that takes you to L'Anse-aux-Meadows, offers other big moments as you head north. First it takes you through Grose Morne National Park where mountains and fjords provide some of the most dramatic scenery in eastern Canada. And halfway to its northern tip it brings you to an archeological site that is actually four times as ancient as the Viking settlement. At the little fishing village of Port au Choix, archeologists unearthed a burial ground of the Maritime Archaic Indians, which tests showed was in use from 2000 to

1200 B.C. The graves, discovered in 1962, turned out to be a gold mine of artifacts made up by these people who had disappeared long before the white man arrived. Searchers found several kinds of harpoons, bone daggers, stone axes, pendants of shells and combs made from bone. Many of the finds are on display at a visitor's interpretation center on this site, which is now a national historic park.

CONTACT

For maps and suggested tour routes, plus an accommodation guide, write to the Newfoundland Department of Tourism, Box 2016, St. John's, Newfoundland A1C 5R8.

For material on Grose Morne and the two archeological sites, contact Parks Canada, Atlantic Region, Historic Properties, Upper Water St., Halifax, Nova Scotia B3J 1S9.

65. Where North America Begins

When the sun rises on North America, fog permitting, its first rays dapple down on the guns of Cape Spear, Newfoundland. This is the easternmost point in North America. Ireland, just 1,640 miles to the east, is actually closer to the cape than is most of the rest of Canada.

Those first rays of a new day also shine down on cliffs that are pock-marked by a rabbit warren of World War II bunkers and on a clifftop lighthouse dating from 1836. The guns aren't nearly that historic; they were installed in 1941 when German submarines threatened Allied shipping at nearby St.

John's harbor. Though Newfoundland was not then a part of Canada, the gun base was manned by Canadian forces stationed, they must have felt, in the world's most godforsaken outpost.

And so it remained long after the war and after Newfoundland entered Confederation. Although it is only 10 miles from downtown St. John's, until a few years ago the road to the cape was so bad that only a few hardy travelers ever used it. Now, there's a good road to the cape and a national historic park is being developed around it and Newfoundland's oldest surviving lighthouse. When the lighthouse began operating on September 1, 1836, sperm whale oil was used to fuel its lights and a system of weights, as in the operation of a grandfather clock, was used to rotate the light. Seal oil, kerosene, pressurized oil vapor and acetylene later supplied the source of light until electricity was installed in 1929. Finally, in 1955 the light was transferred to a nearby tower and the old lighthouse was to be demolished. But concern for its historic worth resulted in protests and it was turned into a historic site.

CONTACT
Parks Canada, 400 Laurier Ave. W., Ottawa, Ontario K1A 0H4 will supply a guide to Cape Spear and the other 55 historic sites in Canada.

66. Uncle Tom's Cabin

We picture Uncle Tom's Cabin beside some cotton field down south. But the original that gave birth to Harriet Beecher Stowe's famous antislavery novel is actually located just a mile west of the little town of Dresden in southwestern Ontario.

A simple wooden structure built with handmade nails about 1842, it was the home of the Reverend Josiah Henson, an escaped slave. Josiah's own life was even more dramatic than the novel. He was born in Maryland and saw his father beaten and sold to an Alabama planter for attempting to protect his mother from a brutal overseer. When Josiah later attempted to buy freedom for himself and his wife and four children, he was tricked out of the money he had saved. He fled with his family to Canada where he attempted to found a colony for escaped slaves.

Harriet Beecher Stowe, who had never been to the South, read a brief account of his life as a slave and arranged a meeting with him. He provided her with much of the material she used as the basis for Uncle Tom. A rocking chair and a few other possessions of the Henson family are on display in the cabin and there is a museum that contains several copies of the Stowe book as well as one that Henson wrote himself.

Henson was accepted as a preacher in the Methodist Episcopal Church and helped found the British American Institute, Canada's first vocational school, to train escaped slaves in useful trades. Buildings used by the school and a church similar to the one Henson preached in are also preserved on the grounds. Henson is buried nearby. The cabin is open daily from May to October. Take Highway 21 north from Highway 401 to reach Dresden.

CONTACT

Ontario Travel, Queen's Park, Toronto, Ontario M7A 2E5 supplies free maps, accommodation guides and a guide to all attractions in the province.

67. Norman Bethune Birthplace

Holidayers heading into the lake-studded Muskoka area of Ontario often pass through the little town of Gravenhurst without realizing that one of its tree-shaded houses is a shrine revered by millions of people. It is the birthplace of Dr. Norman Bethune, a Canadian doctor who is regarded as a martyr in the Republic of China. Chinese diplomats who come to Canada invariably ask to see Dr. Bethune's house.

Always an irascible and controversial character, Bethune became a Communist during the Great Depression of the 1930s and went to Spain to take part in the civil war on the side of anti-Franco Republicans. Here he set up the first mobile blood transfusion unit designed to treat soldiers on the battlefield, a system that was to save thousands of lives during World War II.

In 1938 he went to China to work with the Chinese Communists who were at that time being besieged by the invading Japanese Imperial Army. He was warmly welcomed by Mao Tse-tung and he marched along with the Eighth Route Army as it battled the Japanese in the mountains. He once worked for sixty-nine hours without stopping, operating on 115 cases. He established both mobile units and hospitals for the Chinese and in selfless devotion would walk a whole day to treat a single wounded soldier. In 1939, while operating on a wounded man without rubber gloves because none were available, he cut his finger and sustained a fatal infection. He died on November 12 at the age of forty-nine.

The federal government acquired Bethune's Gravenhurst birthplace in 1973 and through Parks Canada operates it as the Norman Bethune Memorial House. The principal rooms have been furnished in the style of the 1890s to recreate their appearance when Bethune was born there, the son of a Presbyterian minister. Bethune's life and works are portrayed on the second floor with large photographs and text, some of it in Chinese. There are pictures of him as a boy posing with his high school soccer team, a self-portrait, photographs of him at the front in both Spain and China and displays of some of the instruments he invented that are still in use.

The Bethune Home is at the corner of Hughson and John streets in Gravenhurst, which is on Highway 11, 100 miles north of Toronto. It is open daily and there is no admission charge.

68. Home of the Mennonites

Canada's horse-and-buggy days are long gone—except in the rich farming area around Kitchener, Ontario. There horses and buggies and horse-drawn farm machinery are a common sight. For this is the home of the Mennonites, a highly religious people who spurn many of our modern ways. Old Order Mennonites, the strictest members of the sect, still go to church and to town by horse and buggy, refuse to put in central heating, indoor plumbing or electricity and stick to the tried-and-true farming methods of their German ancestors—which don't permit the use of tractors and other modern machinery. They believe strongly in the separation of church and state and refuse military service or government aid of any kind. They live their lives by the doctrine of love and nonviolence taught by Menno Simons, a Roman Catholic priest who broke away from the Church in 1536 and became a leader of the reform-minded Anabaptist movement from which the Mennonites sprang. They were so persecuted in Europe that they were forced to hide in caves; many of them fled to the New World, coming to Pensylvania at the invitation of William Penn. From there, thousands of Mennonites made their way to the rich farmlands of Ontario. They are now one of the most respected religious groups in the province.

You will easily recognize members of the Old Order Mennonite sect. The women wear black bonnets, long homemade dresses and aprons, while the men dress in somber, collarless suits. It is largely because of their influence that Kitchener has two of the finest farmers' markets you will find anywhere in North America. At both the Farmers' Market at Duke and Frederick streets in Kitchener and the smaller but more rustic Waterloo Market on Highway 85, north of the city, you will find homemade sausages, spiced cheeses, apple butter, strudel, maple syrup, sauerkraut and shoofly pie, all sold amid stall after stall of fresh vegetables and fruit. Early Saturday morning is the best time to visit.

In the village of St. Jacobs, on Highway 85 north of Kitchener, you can visit the Meeting Place, a small Mennonite museum with illustrations and taped commentaries explaining the sect's way of life and the reasons for it. In the section of Waterloo county north of the city, you will also come on the white frame meeting houses of Old Order Mennonites which are surrounded by horses and buggies on a Sunday morning. Highways in this part of the country have especially wide shoulders to accommodate this traffic. You can still see the buggies being made and repaired in a large barn on Highway 86, called Simeon's Buggy Works. It's near the town of Elmira, a leading Mennonite center. Elmira holds a huge maple sugar festival each spring with flapjacks being served up all along the main street.

There are, of course, more modern members of the Mennonite sect around Kitchener who use tractors and drive cars. But even some of them paint the shiny bumpers black, as Mennonites shun mirrors and other shiny things that may lead to vanity.

CONTACT
You can get information on the Mennonites by writing to the Kitchener Chamber of Commerce, 67 King St. E., Kitchener, Ontario N2H 6M2.

All across Canada there are marvelous reconstructions of fortresses, gold-rush towns and nineteenth-century villages designed to give a visitor some idea of what life was like at various stages in the country's history. Many are peopled by guides and artisans dressed in period costumes.

Barkerville in British Columbia's caribou country

is a rebuilt ghost town that takes you back to the gold-rush days of the 1860s when a man paid $10 for a single dance with a hurdy-gurdy girl. Old Fort Edmonton on the North Saskatchewan River just outside the Alberta capital recreates the Hudson's Bay post where the city began. It not only shows how the post factor and his family lived but also how they cheated the Indians out of their furs.

In Batoche, Saskatchewan, 30 miles south of Prince Albert, you can visit the battlefield of the last Riel Rebellion and still see the scars on the exterior walls of St. Antoine de Padoue rectory made by the gatling gun, the forerunner of the machine gun that was tried out for the first time in this 1885 battle. And in Manitoba, you can take a 10-mile drive north from Winnipeg to Lower Fort Garry on the banks of the Red River. It is the only stone fort from the fur-trade days that still remains in its original condition.

Ontario has several fine reconstructions depicting different periods in her history. Old Fort William at Thunder Bay takes you back to the early years of the nineteenth century when the trappers from across the west and fur traders gathered for the Great Rendezvous. Sainte-Marie among the Hurons near Midland has risen again. It was the first white settlement in what is now Ontario, a mission from which Jesuits tried to convert the Huron people living there in the seventeenth century. Upper Canada Village, near Morrisburg, is a collection of mid nineteenth-century houses and barns, plus a school, mill, blacksmith shop, cheese factory and church, all adding up to a typical village of the last century.

In Quebec, Old Montreal and the Place Royale section of Quebec city are among the best restorations you will find anywhere in North America. They are also the sites of some of Quebec's best restaurants. In New Brunswick, King's Landing, 23 miles west of Fredericton, is a fine collection of 50 vintage buildings recreating a village that may have existed between 1790 and 1870. Newfoundland's most famous restoration precedes all the others by many centuries. It is the Viking village at L'Anse-aux-Meadows, mentioned earlier, that dates from the year 1000.

69. Fortress Louisbourg

But none of the other reconstructions come close to matching the magnificence of Fortress Louisbourg, located on the often fog-bound coast of Cape Breton Island, 23 miles southeast of Sydney, Nova Scotia. The French built it, starting in 1713. They intended it to be the mightiest military base in North America. So much money from the treasury of France was poured into its construction that Louis XV once complained that he expected to wake up one day in Paris and see Louisbourg rising on the horizon. Its reconstruction was undertaken partly as a project to find jobs for unemployed Cape Breton coal miners and has been just as expensive although only about one-fifth of the original has been restored—some 50 buildings in all. You can visit the elegance of Bourbon France in the governor's quarters of the King's bastion with its rich tapestries, elegant period furniture and fine chinaware and then step into the barracks of the ordinary soldier who slept on straw and dreamed of somehow getting back to France.

Unfortunately for Louisbourg's survival, it's defenses were all geared to an attack from the sea. It fell twice, the first time to an invading force from New England. (The fact that Louisbourg was returned to France after its first surrender is usually listed among the causes of the America Revolution.) When it fell for the last time to the British in 1758, its 2,000 inhabitants were sent home and the British leveled it with explosives. There it lay, little more than a sheep pasture, for more than two centuries until 1961 when it became Canada's most ambitious reclamation. More than $25 million has been spent so far to bring Louisbourg back to life.

In today's Louisbourg, costumed characters dry cod on the beach and bake bread in the beehive ovens of the garrison bakery. Women roast meat over open hearths and make soap and candles while their children roll hoops down the cobblestoned streets. You can sit down in a French colonial tavern for lunch, eating with only a knife, or go next door to the more dignified L'Epee Royalle where ship captains and officers dined when this remote corner of nowhere was the fourth busiest port in North America.

Fortress Louisbourg is open daily from June 1 to September 30. Admission is $2 for adults, 50 cents for children and $4 for family groups. There are 2 small establishments in the town of Louisbourg offering accommodation and there are campgrounds nearby. However, most visitors spend the night in Sydney.

Canada boasts many magnificent churches that will remind a visitor of the great cathedrals of Europe. Almost everyone who visits Montreal, for example, will take in Notre Dame Church, dating from 1829, filled with priceless works of art, capable of holding 5,000 worshipers and topped off with a main bell that weighs 24,780 pounds.

70. The World's Smallest Church

That bell alone is larger than the first of our unusual churches, located in the town of Emo in lake-studded northwestern Ontario, near the Minnesota border. It is just 8 feet by 10 and stands only 36 feet high. It can accommodate only 8 worshipers at a time. Townspeople say it is the world's smallest church. It was built in 1971 on the grounds of St. Patrick's Catholic Church, which burned down the same year.

71. St. Boniface Cathedral

Three years earlier, another fire destroyed the much more famous St. Boniface Cathedral in a French-speaking enclave of the same name that is now a part of Winnipeg. The beloved old walls of the cathedral have been left standing like a Roman ruin while a starkly contemporary new cathedral has been erected within. In the graveyard in front of this shrine, you will find the grave of Louis Riel, who was brought back to his native heath for burial after being hanged in Regina following the failure of the second western rebellion which he led in 1885.

72. Christ Church Cathedral, the Haunted Church

Our third church is also a cathedral, the first to be founded on British soil since the Norman conquest. Christ Church Cathedral was consecrated in Fredericton, New Brunswick, in 1853. What sets it aside from other Canadian churches is the claim that it is haunted by one of Florence Nightingale's nurses. Dozens of people swear they have seen this ghost. All describe her as entering the cathedral by its west door in old-fashioned nurse's togs. No one, however, could say whether or not she was carrying a lamp. Why she haunts the church none can say. But oldtimers who have spotted her were able to identify her as the wife of John Medley, first bishop of the cathedral. Mrs. Medley did, in fact, train with the great Florence.

The cathedral is a truly handsome Gothic structure, containing a facsimile of Big Ben in London that actually predates the famed Westminster timepiece. It was designed by Lord Grimthorpe, perhaps as a working model of the one that has become a symbol of the British capital—but Fredericton's came first. The cathedral stands right in the heart of one of Canada's most beautiful small cities. Just across the way is The Green, a parkland that fronts on the tranquil St. John River. Beside it is one of the many fine gifts with which Lord Beaverbrook, the British press baron and Churchill's wartime confidant who grew up in New Brunswick, endowed the provincial capital. The Beaverbrook Gallery houses one of the finest art collections you'll find anywhere in Canada, with Gainsboroughs, Turners, Reynolds and a gigantic Salvador Dali, measuring 10 by 13½ feet, showing Saint James riding into heaven on horseback. The gallery also contains Graham Sutherland's controversial portrait of Churchill and some watercolors by Sir Winston himself.

CHAPTER XIV

Natural Wonders

73. On Safari in Darkest Ontario

You don't have to go to Africa to go on safari. Lions, cheetahs, elephants, giraffes, baboons, rhino and gazelles are among the 1,000 exotic animals that now roam the grasslands of Ontario at the African Lion Safari park.

The 100-acre preserve, near the village of Rockton, is one of several big-game parks that have been established in North America and Europe to meet the growing public demand for close-ups of these glamorous beasts in wide-open spaces. In safari parks, you wind through various preserves in your car while animals roam about you—and in the case of baboons, right on top of you. A series of fences divides the animals into compatible groups, or at least into groups that won't attack each other. At Rockton, this makes for some pretty strange bedfellows as baboons find themselves sharing their territory with 300-pound black bears. Unlike many other safari parks, the Rockton preserve is located in an area that gets fairly severe winters, with plenty of snow and January and February nights that generally drop well below the freezing point. Ironically, the lions, which adapt by growing long coats, seem to thrive in the cold and look much healthier than they do in summer when you are more apt to get a yawn than a roar out of them. Park manager Don Dailley has a ready explanation for this. "It's not nearly so important to know where an animal came from immediately as it is to know where his predecessors were living at the time of the last ice age when you are trying to figure out whether he'll be able to stand our cold."

Not all conservationists are happy with these game parks. I once interviewed the late Joy Adamson, of *Born Free* fame, at her home in Kenya. She said she had seen safari parks on her North American visits but resented the fact that they afforded animals such as the timid cheetah so little privacy. But Dailley points out that his park now has a reserve away from the viewing areas where mating cheetahs are kept. Cheetahs usually refuse to breed in captivity but the Rockton park has already had some baby cheetahs born there, though none has so far managed to survive. Still, safari park managers believe they can play a conservationist role that zoos can't because the large areas they provide and the large numbers of animals they support allow game to breed by natural selection. Moreover, taking into account the rate at which poachers and urban sprawl are wiping out wildlife in Africa, safari parks are beginning to look more important all the time. They certainly give you the feeling of being close to nature—too close, in some cases. The last time I visited the park, I was driving behind a group in a station wagon who ignored posted warnings and rolled down their windows to feed the baboons. Suddenly, a large black bear came bounding out of the bush to get his share. The windows shot up but that didn't stop bruin from giving the car a shake to show his displeasure. And monkeys have been known to tear the vinyl rooftops off cars when drivers stopped their handouts. But the people actually constitute a greater danger to the animals than the animals do to them. An autopsy on an ostrich that died suddenly in the park some time ago showed it had swallowed the metal tab from a beer or pop can.

If the thought of driving the family car through territory ruled over by the king of the beasts and his cousins doesn't sound like your cup of courage, you can park your car on a large lot inside the gates and ride a double-decker safari bus, complete with guide's commentary, through the wildlife compounds. The park also has an amusement ride area, restaurants and a birds-of-prey exhibit, featuring eagles, hawks, vultures and falcons that reach speeds up to 75 mph when their handler demonstrates their hunting ability by whirling a feathered bait on a string around his head. This may be the only place in the world with signs warning that "Trespassers Will Be Eaten."

CONTACT

Write for brochures to African Lion Safari, Rockton, Ontario L0R 1X0. Admission is $4 for adults, $3 for youth and $2 for children 3 to 12. The park is open daily March through November and on weekends December through February.

74. Flowerpot Islands

Of all the oddities of nature resulting from the fact that the Bay of Fundy has the world's highest tides, the flowerpot islands on New Brunswick's Hopewell Cape are the most curious. They constitute one of the truly unusual places in the Maritimes and no visitor should miss them.

The Fundy tides, which can reach more than 50 feet because of the funnel shape of the bay, create two other minor wonders. At Saint John, the mighty tides rush in to force water back up a small falls, thereby creating the Reversing Falls. And at Moncton, the Petitcodiac River empties and fills twice a day with the ebb and flow of the tide. This phenomenon is known as the Tidal Bore, and is, indeed, Canada's best-named tourist attraction. People come from across the continent to see it, expecting a wall of water to come rushing up the riverbed. Instead, they usually see a ripple that doesn't even force the seabirds feeding there to move.

No such disappointment with nature's quirks occurs at Hopewell Cape, however. There, 300 million years of natural forces have gone into the creation of the numerous pillars of rock, each more than 100 feet high, with trees and shrubs growing atop them as if they were flowerpots set out in the sun. Many visitors think the tides alone created these flowerpots, but that is not the case. In prehistoric times, boulders and gravel were carried down by mighty streams flowing from the nearby Caledonia Mountains. Over millions of years this residue was compressed into a rock known as conglomerate.

Then came glaciers, enlarging fractures in the rock. When the last glaciers retreated 10,000 years ago, the sea took over, washing out the loose rubble and leaving mighty columns of firmer conglomerate standing off the cliffs like sentries.

New Brunswick has now developed The Rocks Provincial Park around the flowerpot area and you can climb down to the base of the cliffs at low tide to explore the pillars and caves carved out by the tides. Some care is needed, of course; loose rock should be avoided and you must be conscious of the fact that the footprints you leave behind in the sand soon will be covered with more than 46 feet of water. It's best to visit during the period 3 hours before to 2 hours after low tide. Times for the tides may be obtained from any New Brunswick Tourist Information Center. The Rocks, which appear to be a series of tiny islets at high tide, are just east of Fundy National Park on Highway 114.

75. Queen Charlotte Islands

Canada ends in the Queen Charlotte Islands, the most westerly point of the country and one of the loneliest. They are so infrequently visited that the British Columbia Ferry Corporation cut off service to the islands some years ago. But, for the man who has been everywhere else, they can be visited fairly easily on daily flights from Vancouver or trips on an amphibian aircraft from nearby Prince Rupert.

The islands have just four motels and a lodge, but you can rent a car at Masset, the largest settlement, and explore both paved highway and logging

Natural Wonders

roads—about 200 miles in all. They take you through rain forests, along miles of lonely beaches and past towering peaks. There are hiking trails in Naikoon Provincial Park, where 15 campsites—usually adequate to handle the crowds—are located at Agate Beach. A potential visitor should be warned that these islands get more than their share of rain but both fresh-water and salt-water fishing is superb. Near Port Clements, you'll find the world's only golden spruce, a 60-foot mutation that has defied attempts to reproduce other trees with similar golden needles.

CONTACT
Tourism British Columbia, 1117 Wharf St., Victoria, British Columbia V8W 2Z2.

76. The Big Fishing Hole

It is estimated that from 12 million to 15 million people a year visit Niagara Falls, so you would hardly consider it part of Offbeat Canada. But hold on! There's an unexpected treat offered there that few visitors ever hear about—one of the world's biggest fishing holes.

After you and your children have seen the falls themselves and the first-rate Marineland and Game Farm show, let them take in some of the countless waxworks and other honkytonk aspects of the falls while you drive north from town along the Niagara Parkway to the vicinity of the famed whirlpool. Park your car in one of the lots and head down to the river, fishing rod in hand. When you reach the bank you'll find a magnificent fishing hole, with sturgeon, chinook and rainbow trout waiting to be taken. A fifty-pound sturgeon was caught recently.

77. The Unknown Spa

British Columbia has Canada's best-known hot springs and spas, with Harrison and Radium Hot Springs attracting an international clientele. But the west coast province also has an interesting hot springs that almost no one knows about. Hot Springs Cove is certainly an unusual place to go to take the waters. Its sulfurous offerings boil forth on the rugged west coast of Vancouver Island in a wilderness surrounded by dense rain forest. The springs bubble out of the earth at more than 85 degrees centigrade and flow down a gully into the ocean. It is estimated that 120 gallons a minute tumble down from the source through a series of pools, with rocky basins getting successively cooler as they near the sea. The highest pool is so hot that it can be used for bathing only in winter when runoff waters mix with those from the springs.

This is a very casual sort of spa. Sneakers are the only clothing required for bathers using the pools, and even they are only necessary because of the occasional sharp rock. Clothes and rain wear are stowed in nearby plastic bags. Some find the atmosphere far too casual while others say it is the best place in Canada to cure arthritis, rheumatism or the blahs of winter.

Unfortunately, no road leads to Hot Springs Cove; you must get there by boat or float plane from the

Natural Wonders

nearby seaside town of Tofino. And the government of British Columbia intends to leave the springs in their wilderness setting as part of Macquinna Provincial Park. The only development in the park is a mile-long trail from the wharf where boats and float planes tie up. There are also a few wilderness campsites.

Most visitors arrive on the float planes run by Pacific Rim Air Lines and McCully Aviation. McCully charges day trippers $40 while people coming for a longer stay can charter a flight for $100 to $150, depending on the number in their party. Canoes can be strapped to the floats of planes for those who want to move around once they arrive.

The Pacific is cold and rough along this coast, crashing against the shore within sight of the bathing pools. Though there is a magnificent, 7-mile beach at nearby Pacific Rim National Park, it is for beachcombing only. Water temperatures rarely rise much above 50 degrees Fahrenheit.

CONTACT

Tourism British Columbia, 1117 Wharf St., Victoria, British Columbia V8W 2Z2 can supply maps and an accommodation guide listing motels at nearby Tofino.

Some of the world's greatest seabird sanctuaries are located along Canada's Atlantic coast. It's not a question of whether or not you'll spot big seabirds in the best of them, but how many thousands will be flying over you at a single time.

78. Bonaventure Island Seabird Sanctuary

That's certainly the case at Bonaventure Island on Quebec's remote Gaspé Peninsula. It is one of the world's largest seabird sanctuaries, with more than 50,000 gannets alone nesting on its cliffs. There are also large colonies of kittiwakes, cormorants, puffins, murres and gulls of every kind. When tour boats approach island cliffs, enough birds fly overhead to darken the sky noticeably.

The gannet, with a wingspan of 6 feet, is one of the most glamorous of all birds and generally puts on a great show for visitors. To the amazement of fishermen, gannets make dives from 400 feet in the air in order to catch fish they spot 50 to 100 feet below the surface. From a tour boat, you can see 10-foot-high splashes all over the bay. The gannet may go several hundred miles out to sea to find good fishing. But when he returns to the cliffs lined with nests it is invariably to the same life-long mate who greets him with great ceremonial caresses.

Most tourists who take in the great show at Bonaventure Island have come to Gaspé in the first place to get a look at Percé Rock, the multicolored, 4-million-ton hunk of limestone that is pierced at one end by a 60-foot-high arch. But the bird show usually turns out to be much more exhilarating. Cruises leave Percé dock at regular intervals during the summer and charge $6 for a return trip to the island. Real bird fanciers can get off at the island on sunny days and walk out to the nesting grounds where protected birds are so tame they will usually pose for closeups. Percé has hillside motels looking out on the pierced rock and the big bird show.

79. Birdwatching on Grand Manan

New Brunswick offers two marvelous birdwatching locations, both of which lie off the main tourist track. Grand Manan, the largest and most remote of the islands in the Bay of Fundy, offers such first-rate birdwatching that even the great John James Audubon raved about it. And if you can't see all 230 species on the wing, you can see them stuffed at the island's Allan Moses Bird Collection museum.

Gulls of every sort and puffins are regulars and whole clouds of sandpipers circle the shoreline. This is one of the few places on earth where the edible seaweed called dulse is harvested commercially. You can see it being gathered at low tide and drying on the beaches. Grand Manan, by the way, is one of Canada's great escape islands. It can be reached only by car ferry from Black's Harbour on the mainland and offers just a couple of hotels, motels, cottages and campgrounds for visitors. Author Willa Cather was among the escapists who spent her summers here.

Expect to pay about $10 for your car and $3 per person for the ferry ride. You can make the return trip in a day and still have a couple of hours to explore the island but its best to plan an overnight stay.

80. Kouchibouguac National Park

More than 200 of the 500 species of birds found in Canada pay summer visits to Kouchibouguac, the national park being developed on New Brunswick's warm Gulf of St. Lawrence shore. There are 150 campsites, a supervised beach, nature trails and birds, birds, birds as the park is on one of the major north-south migratory bird flyways. Flycatchers, herring gulls, ruddy turnstones, chimney swifts, catbirds, cowbirds and killdeers are among the colorful cast of characters spotted in this 93-square-mile nature preserve.

81. Witless Bay Islands Seabird Sanctuary

Two topnotch Newfoundland seabird sanctuaries are within an easy drive of St. John's, the provincial capital. If you can visit only one, drive 25 miles south of St. John's on Route 10 to the Witless Bay and ask a local fisherman to take you out to the Witless Bay Islands Seabird Sanctuary. The price will be right and it will be a trip any nature lover will remember for years. The sanctuary comprises Gull, Green and Great Islands. From mid June to mid July, gannets, puffins and kittiwakes nest on all three islands in the tens of thousands. It is possible to get permits to land on the island by writing to the Director of Wildlife, Department of Tourism, Building 810, Pleasantville, St. John's, Newfoundland.

82. Cape St. Mary's

The other fine seabird sanctuary is 120 miles from the capital at Cape St. Mary's, on the southwest tip of the Avalon Peninsula. The gannet colony there is second in size only to the one at Bonaventure Island.

83. Jack Miner Bird Sanctuary

Ontario also has a special place for nature lovers hoping to get a look at birds on a grand scale. The Jack Miner Bird Sanctuary near Kingsville was one of the first sanctuaries created in North America. It was established by Jack Miner, who at one time well may have been the world's most famous conservationist. He was certainly one of the first. In 1902 he dug a pond on his property and succeeded in raising three ducks. Two years later he adopted three mallards from a local marsh.

At first he kept the ducks as pets, clipping their wings so they couldn't fly away. Then he decided he would rather let them be free and released them to join the normal bird migration south. When several ducks returned to his pond the next spring, he began to wonder if they were the ones he had released. To find out, he decided to capture and to band them so he would know in future years if his own birds kept returning.

He started by patiently trying to coax the ducks to eat from a long-handled spoon and finally succeeded in capturing one, which he named Katie. He scratched his name and address on a small piece of aluminum and attached it to the duck's leg. A month after he released her Katie was shot in South Carolina by a hunter who returned the tag to Miner. Later it became evident to Miner that such taggings would allow him to trace the migratory paths of ducks and geese. Being deeply religious, he began putting a verse of scripture on the tags as well as his name. As a result, many missionaries in Canada's far north sent back the tags given to them by Eskimos and Indians who had killed the birds for food.

To finance his feeding of the birds and his tagging system, Miner began to give lectures in 1910 and, as the father of a romantic new field called conservation, was able to fill large auditoriums. His success as a speaker enabled him to establish the most popular halfway house for birds flying to Canada's far north in spring and to the southern U.S. in autumn. It is still operated today by his family at Kingsville, a tiny community located near the southernmost point of Canada (actually on the same latitude as northern California). It is about 240 miles west of Toronto.

In accordance with his wishes, the Jack Miner sanctuary is closed on Sundays. The best time to see mass bird migrations there is usually during early May and the last two weeks of October.

CONTACT
Jack Miner Migratory Bird Foundation, Kingsville, Ontario.

84. Going Underground

Putting on a hard hat and going down into a mine is anything but fun for the men who have to do it for a living. But for the tourist, it can be a highlight of his trip.

Unfortunately, opportunities to do so are extremely limited; maintaining mine safety is a difficult enough job without having tourists around to worry about. Nevertheless, in 1980 Falconbridge Nickel Mines, near Sudbury in northern Ontario, began offering free guided mine tours in summer to visitors 16 years old and over. The mine is located in the world's largest deposit of nickel and tourists go several hundred feet below ground to see miners at work. Guides take people in groups of 10 on the underground tours, starting at 9:30 A.M. and 1:30 P.M. The mine needs at least a day's notice to include you on a tour. You can call at 705-693-2761. Then all you have to do is drive to the mine's visitors' center in Falconbridge where you will be issued a hard hat and goggles.

In the coal mining region of Cape Breton, the Princess Tourist Mine at Sydney has been taking visitors below for several years now. The mine actually ceased operations in 1975, perhaps to the relief of miners who were by then going 2,000 feet deep and 6 miles out under the ocean to the nearest face of coal. Now visitors are issued hard hats and protective clothing and taken 682 feet down with a retired miner leading them. In the well-lit tunnels he spins tales of underground horror and courage and answers all questions. The tour costs adults $4 and children $2.

In nearby Glace Bay, there's the excellent Miners' Museum, which also offers a mine tour.

CHAPTER XV

Festivals and Other Special Events

Canada offers unique festivals, summer theater that is unmatched anywhere else in North America and historic sports events. In June, you can buy a passport in Toronto that allows you to taste the food, drink and culture of 50 different ethnic groups in a single week. In July you can see the world's greatest bathtub race when real-life rub-a-dub-dubs go to sea at Nanaimo in the big annual race across the Strait of Georgia to Vancouver. In the winter you can attend a northern Mardi Gras or watch a horse race on ice.

85. Metro International Caravan

Toronto goes on its best fun binge in the last nine days of June when the Metro International Caravan takes place. Some 50 pavilions are set up in community halls, church basements, abandoned warehouses and the like by various ethnic communities in this highly cosmopolitan city that is more of a tossed salad than a melting pot. You buy a passport for $6 that enables you to visit any pavilion you wish to try out the souvlaki, borscht, sauerbraten, sashimi or fagioli all'uccelletto. Each pavilion puts on entertainment that ranges all the way from intricate Philippine dances to those rousing Cossack ones where high-booted dancers leap clear across the stage. Some of the entertainment is so professionally done that people line up around the block to get into the most popular pavilions. You can drive or walk between pavilions or take special Caravan buses that follow a continuous route between them. Each pavilion stamps the passport you buy; the passport contains a map locating the various stops on your abbreviated around-the-world journey.

CONTACT
You can get details by writing Metro International Caravan, 263 Adelaide St. W., Tortonto, Ontario M5H 1Y2.

86. World Championship Bathtub Race

The World Championship Bathtub Race from Nanaimo to Vancouver has been held annually for the past twenty years; people come all the way from Australia to compete. Bathtubs are equipped with outboard motors but still prove ungainly enough to produce a kind of modern-day Laurel and Hardy episode. Band concerts, Indian pageants and parades are all part of this week-long mid-July show.

Festivals and Other Special Events 143

87. Quidi Vidi Lake Regatta

The big festive day in St. John's, Newfoundland celebrates North America's oldest sporting event—the regatta on Quidi Vidi Lake. It is held on the first Wednesday in August if the weather is good or on the next suitable day if it is not. The whole city of St. John's takes off to attend the regatta.

88. The Queen's Plate

Another historic Canadian sports event is the Queen's Plate, the oldest annual horse race in North America, predating even the Kentucky Derby. It is held at Woodbine Racetrack in the northwest corner of Metro Toronto, usually on the last Saturday in June. It often attracts royal personages, including the Queen herself on a couple of occasions. The 1981 Plate will be the 122nd edition.

89. The Canadian Club Classic

Ottawa holds a much more offbeat horse race during its mid-February Winterlude festival. Trotting horses race on the frozen surface of the Rideau Canal in the Canadian Club Classic. You have to bundle up for this one because Ottawa is usually in its annual deep freeze in February but it is one of Canada's most colorful events with crowds lining the borders of the canal while the trotters dash along the ice as if they were on a regular track. The surface they race on, by the way, is part of the world's longest ice rink during winter in Ottawa, with more than seven miles of the canal being cleared for skaters.

90. Shakespeare and Shaw

Two of the world's best drama festivals take place in Ontario during the summer. At Stratford, the annual Shakespearean Festival running from early June through October attracts world class actors—Maggie Smith, Siobhan McKenna, Peter Ustinov, James Mason—and more than 500,000 people for its presentation of plays by the Bard and others. Meanwhile, in the Georgian splendor of Niagara-on-the-Lake, the summer Shaw Festival (from June to early October) packs two theaters for works by Shaw and his contemporaries.

91. The Trial of Louis Riel

These two get most of the publicity but you will find several other summer theater presentations of interest in many parts of the country. In Regina, where they hanged the most controversial figure in Canadian history, Louis Riel, you can decide for yourself whether justice was done by attending the annual reenactment of *The Trial of Louis Riel* in July and August on Tuesdays, Wednesdays and Fridays in Saskatchewan House.

Other annual summer theater events include the Four Seasons Musical Theatre in Victoria; Vancouver's Theatre Under the Stars, outdoors in Stanley Park; outdoor musicals at Winnipeg's Rainbow Stage in Kildonan Park; Festival Lennoxville, which presents drama and comedy each summer in Quebec's Eastern Townships, and the everlastingly popular Charlottetown Festival, where *Anne of Green Gables* and several other musicals are presented from late June to late September in the vast Confederation Centre for the Arts. Banff holds an annual Festival of Arts from the end of May to late August to showcase the work of young people who attend the Banff School of Fine Arts. There are chamber recitals, concerts, readings by guest authors, plays and exhibitions of paintings, sculpture and other crafts.

CONTACT
You can get details of this year's offerings from the Festival Office, the Banff Centre, Box 1020, Banff, Alberta T0L 0C0.

Festival Ottawa, which runs through most of July, offers a rich menu of opera and symphony, with a different theme each year. All performances take place in the National Arts Centre.

CONTACT
Details may be obtained from Festival Ottawa, National Arts Centre, Ottawa, Ontario K1R 5W1.

It's not at all on a par with Cannes, but the World Film Festival in Montreal in late August is one of the largest in North America with screenings of new films for spectators held in two large downtown theaters.

CONTACT
Details from World Film Festival, 1455 Boulevard de Mainsonneuve W., Montreal, Quebec H3G 1M8.

92. Old Time Fiddlers Contest

Shelburne, Ontario, is a town of 2,900 that slumbers most of the year. But for one weekend in early August it goes on a foot-stompin' binge that is literally heard across the country.

For the past thirty years, Shelburne has hosted the Canadian Old Time Fiddlers contest which started in an argument between a vintage fiddler and a young upstart over who got the best music out of the much-maligned scratchbox. It began with only 50 contestants and a small pack of friends but now draws 225 contestants from across Canada and the U.S. and crowds of more than 10,000 spectators. And the whole thing is heard across the country on CBC radio. There are contests for the over 65s and youngsters under 12 and a prize of $1,500 is up for grabs in the overall championship class. Wouldn't you know it in these days of Women's Lib, a female fiddler won it for the first time in 1979. Main events are held in the town's arena but there is music on every street corner and at every campsite during the weekend. There are also parades, antique shows and beer gardens.

CONTACT
The contest is always held early in August but dates change from year to year. Ontario Travel, Queen's Park, Toronto, Ontario M7A 2E5, can supply exact dates as well as maps and accommodation guides. Shelburne is about 70 miles northwest of Toronto.

93. Calgary Stampede

Out west, the biggest show is still the Calgary Stampede with bronc riding, chuck wagon races and flapjack breakfasts on downtown streets. It is held for 9 days starting in the second week of July. To the north, Klondike Days in Edmonton celebrate that city's role as the place where many sourdoughs gathered to head for the gold fields in '98. People dress in gay-nineties style and Vegas-style gambling is allowed during the festival that usually follows the dates of the Stampede so you can visit both on a trip to Alberta.

94. Quebec Winter Carnival

Events in Canada, however, aren't just a summertime thing. Some of the country's best happenings occur in other seasons. The closest thing the country has to a Mardi Gras is the Quebec Winter Carnival which starts on the first Thursday in February and runs for 10 days. Big events are usually clustered around the two weekends of the carnival—with ice canoe races across floes of the St. Lawrence River, a world-class parade through the narrow streets of the old city, motorcycle races on ice, streets of ice sculpture, a pee-wee hockey tournament and plenty of boozing. It may well be Canada's most joyful event and besides it is held in her most charming city, Quebec city.

The Pas in Manitoba also holds a colorful winter festival, featuring the world of the trapper complete with dogsled and snowmobile races. Most small towns in Ontario and Quebec also hold winter carnivals in February. You can check with provincial tourist offices for a list.

In spring there are maple sugar festivals in Quebec and Ontario, usually in late February or early March. One of the sweetest is at Elmira, Ontario, in the heart of Mennonite country. It features trips on horse-drawn sleighs into the sugar-bush and outdoor pancake stalls on the main street of town.

Also worth a spring gander on a trip to Ontario is the May blossom festival in the Niagara Peninsula fruit-growing area. On some country roads through the region you don't need rose-colored glasses to see a rose-colored world.

95. Oktoberfest

In the fall, the biggest Oktoberfest this side of Germany is held at Kitchener, Ontario. It is an 8-day spree in the second week of October with beer gardens, oom-pah-pah bands and a big parade. A few weeks earlier you can attend the Grape and Wine Festival in the Niagara Peninsula wine-growing region—9 days of parades, wine-tasting and the like.

96. The World's Biggest Annual Fall Fair

The world's biggest annual fall fair takes place in Toronto from mid August to Labor Day, when the Canadian National Exhibition is held at a permanent exhibition grounds just a stone's throw from downtown skyscrapers. The "Ex" mixes agriculture, modern living exhibits, grandstand and water shows and a gigantic midway into a multi-million-dollar extravaganza.

Just about every small town in Ontario holds a fall fair, in much the same way as nearly every fishing village in the Maritimes has a lobster festival in summer and many prairie cattle towns hold rodeos.

Among the kooky events are the August frog races in St. Pierre-Joys, Manitoba and the turtle derby in Bopssevain, in that same province, in mid August. Regina holds a Buffalo Days celebration around the first of August to celebrate the fact that thousands of these creatures once roamed the area when it was known as Wascana (Pile of Bones). However, none of these is more unusual than the Midnight Golf Tournament held in mid June in Yellowknife where tee-off time is midnight. No one plays in the dark, of course, because Yellowknife in early summer is truly the Land of the Midnight Sun.

CONTACT

Here is a list of government tourist offices from which you can get a calendar of events for each province as well as accommodation and attraction guides, free maps and special information:

Travel Alberta, Box 2500, Edmonton, Alberta T5J 0H4.
Tourism British Columbia, 1117 Wharf St., Victoria, British Columbia V8W 2Z2.
Manitoba Department of Tourism, 200 Vaughan St., Winnipeg, Manitoba R3C 1T5.
New Brunswick Department of Tourism, Box 12345, Fredericton, New Brunswick E3B 5C3.
Newfoundland Department of Tourism, Box 2016, St. John's, Newfoundland A1C 5R8.
Nova Scotia Department of Tourism, Box 456, Halifax, Nova Scotia B3J 2R5.
Ontario Travel, Queen's Park, Toronto, Ontario M7A 2E5.
Prince Edward Island Department of Tourism, Box 940, Charlottetown, Prince Edward Island C1A 7N5.
Ministere de Loisir, de la Chasse et de la Pêche, Direction des Communications, Case postale 22000, Quebec G1K 7X2.

Sask Travel, 3211 Albert St., Regina, Saskatchewan S4S 5W6.
TravelArctic, Yellowknife, Northwest Territories X1A 2L9.
Tourism Yukon, Box 2703, Whitehorse, Yukon Y1A 2C6.

CHAPTER XVI
Getting Around

97. Jet Holidays

When people dream of jet-set holidays, exotic faraway places are usually the subject matter. But within the past couple of years, Canada has come up with some intriguing airline holiday packages, too. A holiday package is one in which your return air trip, your accommodation at the other end, transfers to and from the airport, sightseeing activities and sometimes meals for a week or two are all lumped together in one overall price. Often a charter flight is used to cut the costs of getting you to your destination.

For years now, such charter holiday packages have flown Canadians off to the Caribbean, Hawaii, Mexico and Florida. Now they can also take you off to the west coast for a sailing holiday amid offshore islands, jet a western Canadian east for a week of houseboating on Ontario's Kawartha Lakes and take you to Alberta for a wrangler holiday in which you spend a couple of days on each of 3 ranches that offer trail riding. Other jet holiday packages take you river rafting or supply you with your own motor home to go exploring. Naturally, there is also a selection of more conventional packages, ones where you fly west for a bus tour of the Rockies and the British Columbia coast or one where you fly east or west and are supplied with a car and vouchers for accommodation once you get there.

The cost of such a holiday package is usually based on 2 people sharing a room. You could expect to pay about $550 each for the wrangler holiday, mentioned above, in which you fly to Calgary and spend a week on 3 ranches. Your air fares, rental car, accommodation and most of your meals are included in the price. For the yacht holiday, it would cost each of 4 people about $570, including the return flight from eastern Canada to Vancouver and the yacht rental.

How do you find out the exact details on such packages? Just contact a travel agent and he will supply you with brochures from several tour companies. You should also ask him for advice on the pros and cons of the various packages available. Last year the most imaginative airline packages were put together by a Toronto company called Chieftain Tours. You can, of course, build a package of your own by seeking out the cheapest air fare to your destination and arranging to rent a motorhome or to book a week of trail riding at the other end, or have a travel agent do this for you.

98. Train Tours

VIA Rail, the government agency that now operates most of Canada's passenger trains, offers dozens of escorted tours to almost every part of the country. Buses are used in combination with trains to give you close-ups of the areas you visit, which could be the Manitoba shores of Hudson Bay, Quebec's Saguenay and Gaspé regions, the Cabot Trail of Cape Breton or the Rockies and the B.C. coast, the latter trip including a ferryboat cruise. Trains are also used in western tours run by major tour companies such as Horizon Holidays and UTL Holiday Tours. All can be booked through travel agents.

99. Nature Tours

Some of the best offbeat tours of Canada are offered through the Federation of Ontario Naturalists and Canadian Nature Federation. The Canadian Nature Tours that they sponsor could take you to the Arctic, houseboating along the Trent, birdwatching in southern Ontario, on a backpacking or canoe trip, horseback riding in the Rockies or on a Hudson Bay photo safari. Naturally, these trips are especially designed for people with a keen interest in wildlife and conservation. Nearly 40 trips within Canada are offered, varying in price from $175 to several thousand dollars. Participants must join either of the 2 sponsoring organizations for a fee of $17.

CONTACT
You can get details from Canadian Nature Tours, 355 Lesmill Rd., Don Mills, Ontario M3B 2W8.

100. Young-Adult Adventures

If you are between 18 and 25, you can join an overland trek across Canada by bus in which you camp along the way. Price is a big feature on these holidays, with all-inclusive costs averaging just over $40 a day. Tour buses generally have a crew of three—a driver, an escort and a cook—and they carry all the equipment you need except a sleeping bag. You are expected to assist in setting up camp, help with the barbecue or lend a hand in cleaning up after meals but you are free to take part in planned activities or go out on your own at stops along the way.

Usually, you pay a basic price for the tour, about $450 for a 13-day, cross-country trip, and put $3 a day into the food kitty for food purchased by the staff as you go along. You also need to carry about $10 a day for nights out, sightseeing extras and lunches. Treks are available on a one-way basis between Toronto and Vancouver or you can do a 26-day round trip, returning through the U.S. Trips can be booked through travel agents; Travel of Toronto is the best known of those in the young-adult market. Wilderness canoe trips are also available.

101. An Exchange Bargain

Schools now arrange excellent exchange programs with students from other areas of the country. But there's one unusual exchange opportunity available to youngsters from 14 to 22 that can be done on an individual basis. It could end up costing just a few dollars, even if the person you exchange with lives in a distant part of the country. It is a government-sponsored program called Open House Canada in which reciprocal exchanges are arranged between young people with common interests. You apply, are given the name and address of a kindred spirit and are then required to correspond for at least 6 weeks with him or her. If the exchange still seems desirable, the program will pay transportation costs with each host family expected to put up the participants free of charge on a reciprocal exchange basis. It costs $10 to take part in the program.

CONTACT
Open House Canada, Department of the Secretary of State, 66 Slater St., Room 2326, Ottawa, Ontario K1A 0M9 will send you an application form.

GETTING AROUND: GENERAL INFORMATION

BY AIR: Though Canadian airlines don't offer quite the variety of air-fare gimmicks available south of the border, there are a number of offbeat ways of getting around Canada. You will, for example, find big discounts available to those who are willing to fly at ungodly hours or to pack their own lunches instead of demanding meal service. The thing to keep in mind is this. No holidayer should pay the regular economy fare for a flight to his destination until he has checked to make sure no discount flight is available. He can do this by checking directly with the airlines or by contacting a travel agent. Tickets purchased through travel agents cost the same as they do bought directly from the airline and a good agent should be ready to advise you on the choices available to any destination.

CP Air operates a SkyBus between Toronto and Montreal and the western cities of Vancouver, Edmonton, Calgary and Winnipeg for less than half the economy fare. No food service is available on SkyBus flights which means you take your own lunch. Also you must put down your money when you buy your ticket and you must go in person to a CP Air office or to a travel agent—no phone reservations are accepted. Air Canada offers several bargain holiday fares, too, though none is as good for summer travel as the SkyBus. Air Canada Nighthawks take you to various major cities around the country using aircraft that previously sat on the tarmac all night. Now they are leaving cities late at night and whizzing people about at 2 A.M. and 3 A.M. For the inconvenience involved, you get to fly at close to half fare.

Air Canada also usually has a spring and autumn seat sale, with low prices offered to passengers flying before and after the summer rush. Both CP Air and Air Canada offer charter-class seats on regular flights to people who book 14 days ahead and stay at their destination no more than 30 days. These charter-class fares are well below regular economy-class rates but are much more expensive than SkyBus or Nighthawks.

Several charter airlines also provide service between major cities, mostly in the summer. Tickets for a charter flight must be booked in advance. Charter companies sometimes offer packaged holidays with their flights but you can also buy just plain transportation. Costs are similar to charter class on scheduled airlines.

On short-range flights, such as between Toronto and Montreal or Ottawa, airlines usually offer bargain fares on weekends when the regular business traffic isn't using planes. You can usually get 30 percent off fares for going on Saturday or Sunday on short hops.

Don't forget to ask about discount fares from lesser-kown airlines flying the same routes as the big boys. Nordair, for example, offers a discount of about 30 percent for anyone who makes a return flight between Toronto and Montreal on the same day. Book early on any bargain-priced flight. In July and August discount flights are often sold out months in advance.

BY CAR: The Trans-Canada Highway, sweeping 5,000 miles across the country from St. John's, Newfoundland, to Victoria, British Columbia is the country's main artery. Hundreds of paved highways branch off it and criss-cross the southern section of the country like a vast spiderweb. Roads in northern Canada, especially the Northwest Territories, are few and far between, with just one road reaching the Arctic and no highways at all to the eastern section of the territories. Expect gravel surfaces when driving in either the Yukon or Northwest Territories. In heavily populated parts of the country, however, you will now find expressways such as Highway 401 in Ontario which is 16 lanes wide at some points.

Keep in mind when crossing the prairies that there is now an alternate route to the Trans-Canada, known as the Yellowhead Highway, which enables you to make a return trip without going back over the same territory. It takes a more northerly course (via Edmonton and Jasper) than the Trans-Canada.

Speed limits vary from province to province, with 50 mph (80 km per hour) limits now in vogue on many highways as a result of the fuel situation. Most highway speed limits are now given in kilometers. To convert roughly to miles simply multiply by 0.6.

BY TRAIN: Most of the country's passenger trains are now operated by VIA, the government agency that took this segment of transportation over from Canadian National and Canadian Pacific railways in 1976. In 1982 the agency will replace some of its aging trains with lighter, faster models known as LRCs. Service is generally good on the busy corridor between Windsor and Quebec city, with high-speed turbo trains involved in some runs. Transcontinental trains running from eastern cities through the Rockies to Vancouver are extremely popular in summer.

Although VIA's service has been the subject of some criticism of late, the agency showed a 20-percent increase in passengers last summer. It offers a selection of package plans, including hotels and sightseeing, on several of its routes. These can be booked through travel agents or by contacting VIA Rail Canada Inc., 20 King St. W., 5th floor, Toronto, Ontario M5H 1C4, with offices in most major cities. In the U.S. VIA bookings can be made through Amtrak.

BY BUS: Frequent service is provided by a variety of bus companies between major cities in all parts of the country and to major resort areas. Bus companies also offer a variety of tours, including day tours that are tied in with another activity such as a boat cruise.

About the Author

Gerry Hall is a former president of The Society of American Travel Writers, and has been a travel writer for sixteen years. He is now travel editor for the *Toronto Star,* and lives with his wife and seven children on a farm in rural Ontario.

Great Reading from SIGNET

- ☐ **THE EBONY TOWER** by John Fowles. (#E9658—$2.95)
- ☐ **THE FRENCH LIEUTENANT'S WOMAN** by John Fowles. (#E9003—$2.95)
- ☐ **FEAR OF FLYING** by Erica Jong. (#E9715—$2.95)
- ☐ **HOW TO SAVE YOUR OWN LIFE** by Erica Jong. (#E7959—$2.50)*
- ☐ **TRIPLE** by Ken Follett. (#E9447—$3.50)
- ☐ **EYE OF THE NEEDLE** by Ken Follett. (#E9550—$3.50)
- ☐ **THE PRIZE** by Irving Wallace. (#E9455—$2.95)
- ☐ **THE CHAPMAN REPORT** by Irving Wallace. (#E9456—$2.95)
- ☐ **THE THREE SIRENS** by Irving Wallace. (#E9457—$2.95)
- ☐ **A GARDEN OF SAND** by Earl Thompson. (#E9374—$2.95)
- ☐ **TATTOO** by Earl Thompson. (#E8989—$2.95)
- ☐ **CALDO LARGO** by Earl Thompson. (#E7737—$2.25)
- ☐ **ON THE ROAD** by Jack Kerouac. (#E8973—$2.50)
- ☐ **THE DHARMA BUMS** by Jack Kerouac. (#J9138—$1.95)

* Price slightly higher in Canada

Buy them at your local
bookstore or use coupon
on next page for ordering.

SIGNET Books for Your Reference Shelf

- ☐ **THE NEW AMERICAN WEBSTER HANDY COLLEGE DICTIONARY.** Over 100,000 definitions in this comprehensive dictionary which includes illustrations, abbreviations, geographical names, and colloquialisms. (#W8790—$1.50)
- ☐ **THE NEW AMERICAN MEDICAL DICTIONARY AND HEALTH MANUAL by Robert E. Rothenberg, M.D., F.A.C.S.** This revised edition includes a complete Medicare Handbook and up-to-date information on contraceptive drugs and devices in addition to over 8700 definitions of medical terms, diseases and disorders, a comprehensive health manual, charts and tables, and much, much more. With over 300 illustrations. (#E8314—$2.50)
- ☐ **A DICTIONARY OF DIFFICULT WORDS by Robert H. Hill.** The essential companion to every abridged dictionary complete with 15,000 entries on business, technology, culture, medicine, science, acronyms, and foreign words. (#J6433—$1.95)
- ☐ **THE NEW AMERICAN ROGET'S COLLEGE THESAURUS in Dictionary Form.** Newly revised and expanded. Now as easy to use as a dictionary—and as important to own—here is a treasure house of words and their synonyms and antonyms listed alphabetically for quick, convenient use. (#J9335—$1.95)
- ☐ **THE CONCISE DICTIONARY OF 26 LANGUAGES IN SIMULTANEOUS TRANSLATION by Peter M. Bergman.** The only comprehensive book of its kind that translates 26 modern languages instantaneously. An imperative volume for college students, travelers, businessmen, readers, and all reference libraries. (#E8312—$2.50)

Buy them at your local bookstore or use this convenient coupon for ordering.

THE NEW AMERICAN LIBRARY, INC.
P.O. Box 999, Bergenfield, New Jersey 07621

Please send me the SIGNET BOOKS I have checked above. I am enclosing $_____(please add 50¢ to this order to cover postage and handling). Send check or money order—no cash or C.O.D.'s. Prices and numbers are subject to change without notice.

Name _____

Address _____

City_____ State_____ Zip Code_____

Allow 4-6 weeks for delivery.
This offer is subject to withdrawal without notice.

World Literature Anthologies from MENTOR

- [ ] **21 GREAT STORIES edited by Abraham H. Lass and Norma L. Tasman.** A collection of the all-time great short stories including the works of Chekov, Pirandello, Saki, Bierce, Poe, De Maupassant, Thurber, Twain and many others.
(#MJ1843—$1.95)

- [ ] **STORIES OF THE AMERICAN EXPERIENCE edited by Leonard Kriegel and Abraham H. Lass.** Vivid insights into American life by some of our greatest writers, including Hawthorne, Melville, Twain, Harte, Crane, Shaw, Steinbeck, Faulker and other outstanding American writers.
(#ME1605—$2.25)

- [ ] **MASTERS OF THE SHORT STORY edited by Abraham Lass and Leonard Kriegel.** Complete with individual biographical and critical forewords, here is a superlative gathering of twenty-seven great stories offering unforgettable insight into the greatness of literature. The great masters included are: Balzac, Pushkin, Poe, Gogol, Flaubert, Broges, Kafka and Camus.
(#ME1744—$2.50)

- [ ] **THE MENTOR BOOK OF SHORT PLAYS edited by Richard H. Goldstone and Abraham H. Lass.** A treasury of drama by some of the finest playwrights of the century that includes Anton Chekhov, Thornton Wilder, Tennessee Williams, Gore Vidal, Terence Ratigan and Paddy Chavefsky.
(#ME1730—$2.25)

- [ ] **THE SECRET SHARER AND OTHER GREAT STORIES edited by Abraham H. Lass and Norma L. Tasman.** Brilliant examples of some of the finest writers such as Prosper Merimee, Bernard Malamud, Dorothy Parker, Willa Cather, and Stephen Vincent Benet.
(#MJ1801—$1.95)

Buy them at your local

bookstore or use the coupon

on the last page to order

SIGNET and MENTOR Books You'll Want to Read

- [ ] **SEVEN LONG TIMES by Piri Thomas.** A searing first-hand account of survival in the hell of maximum security prison. "As moving as it is trenchant... every bit as compelling as the author's *Down These Mean Streets!*"—*Publishers Weekly* (#ME1439—$1.75)

- [ ] **IF THEY COME IN THE MORNING by Angela Y. Davis and other political prisoners.** Foreword by Julian Bond. The essays and poetry in defense of the American political prisoner. (#Y4999—$1.25)

- [ ] **MANCHILD IN THE PROMISED LAND by Claude Brown.** The provocative bestselling autobiography revealing the spirit of a new pioneering generation of blacks in the North who have entered the mainstream of American society as a determined, aggressive, hopeful people. (#E8206—$1.75)

- [ ] **HOWARD STREET by Nathan C. Heard.** A raw, powerful picture of ghetto life, this novel gives a shocking insight into the lives of the lost souls who live there... "Nathan C. Heard obviously knows it stone cold."—*N.Y. Times* (#E9542—$2.50)

- [ ] **SOME KIND OF HERO by James Kirkwood.** A novel of our times by the bestselling author of P.S. YOUR CAT IS DEAD. "A portrait of modern heroism, of some kind of hero, our American, contemporary kind: caught in a war, ambiguous about himself, close to crime, yet never far from compassion and deep love!"—*Washington Post* (#E9850—$2.75)

Buy them at your local

bookstore or use coupon

on last page to order

MENTOR Titles You'll Enjoy

☐ **LEISURE: THE BASIS OF CULTURE by Josef Pieper.** In a series of astonishing essays, the author indicts the 20th-century cult of "work" and hectic amusements, which can ultimately destroy both our culture and ourselves. Introduction by T. S. Eliot. (#MW1723—$1.50)

☐ **GREAT DIALOGUES OF PLATO translated by W. H. D. Rouse.** A new translation into direct, forceful modern English of *The Republic* and other dialogues. (#ME1803—$2.95)

☐ **UNDERSTANDING ORIENTAL PHILOSOPHY by James K. Feibleman.** The essential introduction to the thought and religions of India, China, and Japan . . . "A lucid unravelling . . . jargon-free and illuminating."—*Publishers Weekly* (#ME1916—$2.50)

☐ **I CHING edited and with an Introduction by Raymond Van Over.** The definitive new rendering of the ancient Chinese book of divination. The classic James Legge version which is the most thorough translation taken directly from the Chinese text, has been newly edited and arranged for maximum ease in consulting the hexagrams. (#ME1842—$2.50)

☐ **TAOIST TALES edited by Raymond Van Over.** The first mystical writings of mankind's religious consciousness—one of China's great contributions to the world. (#ME1650—$2.25)

Buy them at your local bookstore or use this convenient coupon for ordering.

THE NEW AMERICAN LIBRARY, INC.
P.O. Box 999, Bergenfield, New Jersey 07621

Please send me the SIGNET and MENTOR BOOKS I have checked above. I am enclosing $_____ (please add 50¢ to this order to cover postage and handling). Send check or money order—no cash or C.O.D.'s. Prices and numbers are subject to change without notice.

Name _____

Address _____

City _____ State _____ Zip Code _____

Allow 4-6 weeks for delivery.
This offer is subject to withdrawal without notice.